To My FRIEND J.

FIND YOUR LANE AND DRIVE
WITH PURPOSE! So HONORED
TO BE ON THIS JOURNEY WITH YOU.
WISHING YOU CONTINUED SUCCESS!

FIND YOUR LANE

BRUCE W

12/2017

"Bruce Waller has been a winner in every lane he has chosen. In *Find Your Lane* he shares compelling personal illustrations and real-world insights that can be quickly applied. A fun, engaging read that delivers what we need to win in our own lives!"

— **Lee J. Colan, Ph.D.**
Author, *The 5 Coaching Habits of Excellent Leaders*

"Bruce's writing is relatable in style, inspirational in content, and applicational in structure. I've seen him apply these principles along his life's journey and achieve great results. He is truly a 'lifter' of others; this book will have that impact upon you, too."

–**Dave Nelson, CRP, GMS-T, RIM, CMC, COIC**
Chief Customer Officer, Armstrong Relocation & Companies

"*Find Your Lane* is an inspiring journey from risking it all to becoming a top performer. Bruce Waller is an encourager; a lifter. He shares his story and much of the wisdom collected on his journey, so that you may be lifted to pursue your dreams and write your story."

–**Mark Waller, CRP, PHR, SHRM-CP**
General Manager, A-1 Freeman North American, Inc.

"If you want to take your life to a higher level, this book is for you. Bruce Waller's story and message is a wonderful example of how to chart life's journey, overcome challenges, and stay committed. He shares his wisdom that comes from a life of integrity, good attitude, and gift of connecting people. His love for life and people is an inspiration; I am proud to be his friend. This book will have a powerful influence on all who read it."

–**Lynne Stewart**
Owner, SUPERIORHIRE

"*Find Your Lane* is a great read. The book is such a perfect reflection of Bruce. His desire to always be his best and perform at the top shows through clearly in *Find Your Lane*."

–Brad C. Shanklin
Executive Director, DallasHR and The HRSouthwest Conference

"True leaders inspire others to grow. Bruce Waller is that kind of leader, inspiring the next generation using his life stories, modern examples, and experiences from other true leaders. If you want to discover your dreams or find your lane in life, follow Bruce's advice and get moving to a more successful you. YOU WILL NOT ONLY FIND YOUR LANE, BUT MAY ALSO FIND YOURSELF IN THE PASSING LANE!"

–Michael Gonzales
President, Armstrong Relocation - Dallas

"*Find Your Lane* will immediately engage you on a journey of personal growth. Bruce Waller reveals his compassion, genuineness, and heart as he shares stories and lessons learned from authors, mentors, family, friends, and life experiences. He generously shares his philosophy of lifelong learning and his ability to assimilate leadership insights into a practical, thought-provoking book."

–Deborah Avrin
Management Skills Resource, Inc.

FIND YOUR LANE

Change Your GPS and Change Your Career

BRUCE W. WALLER

Cover design by Melinda R. Prescott
Edited by LeAnn H. Gerst

Printed in the United States of America.
First edition 2017.

ISBN-13: 978-0692865637

www.brucewaller.com

To my wife Dana and my wonderful children,
for the joy you have given me
and continue to give me each day.
I pray every day that you find the lane that
gives you greatest joy in your life.

Special thanks to Lee J. Colan, Deborah Avrin, Mark Waller, Lynne Stewart, Joe Waller, Tony Bridwell, Chrissy Conner, Deanna Huff, Morgan Myers, Steve Laswell, Deborah Reynolds, and so many others in my network for investing time in this project to provide feedback, advice, and inspiration to keep me pushing ahead.

Special thanks to LeAnn Gerst for helping me bring this book to life, and to Melinda Prescott for designing the book cover. I couldn't imagine completing this project without including you on my journey. Thank you both for your creativity and continuous encouragement.

You are all great lifters and have been my fuel to keep going. I appreciate the opportunity to be in the same lane with you while on this great journey.

CONTENTS

There are moments in life that mark time in a special way. A wedding day, the birth of a child, the first time you bowled a perfect game, and the moment you meet someone who is a true difference maker. The closest I will ever get to a 300 in bowling is by adding up three games in a row. So, three out of four isn't bad for me.

Over the years it has been my privilege and honor to encounter some amazing people in my line of work. One such person has been Bruce Waller. The first time I met Bruce was like meeting an old friend you haven't seen in a few years. There is something magnetic about a person who is deeply interested in serving the needs of others. Knowing Bruce was from my home state of Oklahoma sealed the deal—I wanted to know more about this guy.

Both Bruce and I quickly realized our connection went deeper than our Oklahoma roots. Bruce's wife, Dana, and I grew up in the same small town of Duncan, Oklahoma, attending the same school much of our life and graduating High School the same year together. The world just continues to get smaller every day.

If we pay close attention as we go through life, we will discover people who come into our lane from time to time to inspire, encourage, and lift us up to new heights. Bruce is one of those people. Within moments of meeting Bruce, you will understand his purpose

—to serve you in a way that lifts you up. Few people have as much passion for people as Bruce Waller.

Bruce expands his servant leadership reach by imparting his common-sense wisdom onto the pages of his first book, *Find Your Lane*. There is an old saying; common-sense is not always common-practice. What I would add is when common-sense becomes common-practice you get uncommon results. Thus, the true power of *Find Your Lane* is in the simple, common-sense approach to leadership.

Too often we overcomplicate every aspect of life. Bruce has reminded me through a powerful collection of stories and insights just how important it is to Grow, Plan, and Share as I continue down my lane in life. One of the primary roles of a leader is to take the complex and make it simple, Bruce has done just that. *Find Your Lane* removes the complexity of living life in what many today consider the fast lane by having the reader "pull over and review."

On every page I caught myself silently nodding my head in agreement, smiling at times, and wiping the moisture from my eyes occasionally. We spend our entire life in one of two roles—we are either leading or following. *Find Your Lane* prepares, reminds, encourages, inspires, and lifts you to master either role in life.

The ten leadership lessons are practical and to the point, allowing the reader to apply what they are learning immediately. While I read this book in one setting I now realize the bigger value is to read and apply a chapter a week allowing myself to go deeper on each leadership lesson, using the summary at the end of each chapter as my guide.

While my bowling game may be just shy of a perfect 300 game, I am more prepared to roll a perfect game in life as will you once you invest in yourself first and *Find Your Lane*.

–Tony Bridwell
Sr. Partner, Partners in Leadership, Inc.

DIFFERENT LANES PROVIDE DIFFERENT RESULTS

"Just keep going. Everybody gets better if they keep at it."

–Ted Williams

I can remember being around the game of bowling since I was about 7 or 8 years old. My mother Martha Ellen Thornton introduced me to the game in Edmond, Oklahoma, at Edmond Lanes, where she eventually met my stepfather Jack Howard Thornton, the bowling proprietor of the center. My mom signed me and my brothers and sisters up for Saturday morning bowling youth leagues when we were kids. One of my first tournaments was in this center with my mom in the mother-son division of the Parent-Child Tournament.

In 1976, my stepfather purchased a 12-lane bowling center in the small town of Seminole, Oklahoma, and moved our family of 7. It was there that I got to experience life in a small town where everyone knew each other. The bowling center was one of the main places in town where people would go to bowl, to play video games and pool, or to enjoy a grilled hamburger and french fries.

When I was 19 years old I rolled my first 300 perfect game in the Monday night men's bowling league. I was bowling anchor (position #5) and it was the first game of the season. It was very exciting and a feeling I won't ever forget. I was using a "Black Hammer" bowling ball and competing on lanes 3 and 4, which were the best lanes in the center for high scores.

Many people are not aware of bowling oil lane patterns, but the lanes are oiled each day, which can make the game super challenging for even the best bowlers. It can also make a very easy scoring condition for those that curve or hook the bowling ball. Some lanes are also easier than others not only because of the oil conditions, but also because some are bowled on more or less than others, and the humidity or air in the center can affect the lane condition as well.

In Seminole, lanes 11 and 12 were the most difficult to score on. There was a large blowing heater that blew over lane 12, which made it extremely dry. This made it difficult to control the curve of the ball. Lane 11, however, was super slick. Achieving a high score required making big adjustments for each lane. My favorite lanes were 3 and 4 because they were right behind the desk and I could often practice on this pair when work was slow.

In 1989, I was competing in the US Open qualifier for a spot to bowl in the US Open as an amateur in Ada, Oklahoma. I was very familiar with this center and knew middle lanes 10 through 18 were the best-scoring lanes in the center. I was excited to find out that my starting position for the tournament was on the lower lanes. This would allow me to bowl one game on a pair of lanes then move to the right. My strategy was to just stay close the first four games over eight lanes, then hopefully catch fire on the last four games where the scoring lanes would be better for my game. This was right on plan as I finished the final game with a perfect score of 300, earning a spot in the finals.

Finding the best lane in bowling is a lot like finding the right lane on the highway. Some people prefer the left lane so that they can travel quickly and pass others who get in their way. Others are more comfortable in the right lane where traffic moves at a slower pace. Both lanes will get you to the same place, but the journey is so much better when you find the lane that works best for you.

This book isn't about bowling or driving, but the analogies are similar to various stages in life. Many people have a great vision of where they want to be in life, but don't know how to get there. Others enjoy success yet feel stuck and need guidance to grow in their professional or personal life.

No matter where you're at in your life's journey, there's always room for improvement. Are you just starting out? Are you stuck or bored in your current role and looking for the next big thing? Are you looking for ways to grow your sales as a salesperson in your company, or move up as a leader in your company? Maybe you're thinking about finishing college or looking for your next job opportunity. You may be closer than you think and just need an idea or strategy to help you find the right lane for success.

One mistake people often make is comparing themselves with other successful people instead of looking to them for inspiration and strategies they can incorporate into their own plan for success. This is one of the reasons I decided to write this book and share it with others—to pass along what I've learned through my journey thus far in hopes to inspire you and get you moving toward your life's purpose. When we find our lane, life is just different. It gives us joy and opportunities to connect with people to share our story and provide inspiration to others.

One of the keys to finding your lane is to identify what's most important to you, and then have the courage to align your next steps with those values. Maybe you're looking for autonomy so that you can make your own schedule. Or an opportunity to lead a team, or a position that allows you to use your creative skills. We are all on a great journey together trying to find our purpose in life.

When you align the various aspects of your life with your values and the things that are most important to you, your relationships will improve and your job will feel more like a calling. Finding your lane isn't always easy—especially if you're just starting out in life. This is because you haven't had a lot of experience with failure. Transitioning from one lane to another can also be difficult if you've been in the same job your entire career and feel unsure of your next calling.

Finding your lane often means making some mistakes, and there may be times when you feel there's no way out. But you have to push through it. The more mistakes you make early on, the more you can learn from them and grow and share your experiences with others. Many people like to stay in the slow lane where they are comfortable and can steer clear of mistakes, but real personal growth happens when you venture out of your comfort zone and into the lane that's meant for you. The choice is yours!

It really is true that once you find your lane, you will not have to work another day in your life. My hope is the leadership lessons shared in this book will change your course and have real impact on both your professional and personal life.

So buckle your seatbelt and get ready to find your lane . . .

CHAPTER 1

It's Not How You Start, But How You Finish

"The secret of getting ahead is getting started."

–Mark Twain

Are you stuck trying to figure out what's next in your career? We all have moments when we look back and think about where we have been and where we want to go on our journey. Many times we don't really get off to a great start due to some of the choices we make. Sometimes it just takes someone in your family or network to share their perspective or idea to ignite a flame for you to move toward your dreams.

Defining Moments

We all have what I call defining moments. One of those defining moments for me came when I was having a conversation with my wife early in our marriage about our future.

We were driving down the highway one afternoon on our way home from visiting our family when my wife asked me if I was planning on finishing college. I had started my journey toward a bachelor's degree about four years earlier when I decided to leave after my freshman year to get married and start a family. Now, two children later, she was curious if I had been thinking about the future or was just going to accept the current situation with no plan in mind.

That was a defining moment for me because I realized that my future was in my control. Have you been in a similar situation? We all have choices to make in life and nobody can make those choices for us but ourselves. It is up to you to take action if you want to make a difference.

I knew going back to college would be difficult as a parent and working full time, but I also knew the importance of finishing school to start a career and raise my family. I didn't start well in college, but I still had a choice to finish well. So I started taking some college classes the following spring. It was challenging at times, but my dream of finishing had been ignited by that one conversation.

Fast forward five years later—I achieved my goal of finishing what I started and graduated with a college degree. My most memorable moment on graduation day was looking across the crowd and seeing my parents, my wife, and my children cheering for me as I walked across the stage to receive my diploma. The feeling of accomplishment I experienced that day from all the hard work and sacrifice that went into achieving my degree was like none other.

Finishing what you start out to accomplish is challenging, but it will also give you great confidence and joy in life for making the choice to finish something worthwhile.

Is there something you set out to pursue in life but didn't finish?

Sometimes it's just a matter of timing, while other times it's an obstacle you need to find a way to get over, around, under, or break through before you experience success. We all have choices in life that can make an impact today. It's never too late to get started!

My brother Mark said something to me one day that has stuck with me for over 20 years. He said, "It's not how you start, but how you finish." Some of the best advice I've ever received.

Doug Sandler once shared a post on Twitter that says it best— "The 10 most powerful two-letter words are "IF IT IS TO BE IT IS UP TO ME."

Sticking With Your Goals and Dreams

Blake Treinen is an inspiring American baseball story and great example of what it means to not worry about how you start, but finding your lane to finish.

Blake Treinen pitched for Osage High School as a freshman, but quit his sophomore year due to developing pre-diabetes. He returned his junior year with a fastball of 79 mph. In 2007, Blake enrolled at Baker College to play college baseball and then transferred to Arkansas in 2008. But Blake didn't get to play baseball. He was denied the opportunity to try out so he began weight training.

During Christmas, Blake decided to attend a baseball camp led by retired MLB pitcher, Don Czyz. He was then recommended to the head coach, Ritchie Price, at South Dakota State University, where he continued his baseball career. With a fastball now averaging around 88 mph, Blake was drafted by the Miami Marlins in the 23rd round of the 2010 draft. Soon thereafter the Marlins withdrew their offer due to Blake's MRI revealing shoulder inflammation. During Blake's senior year of college, his fastball was clocked as high as 97 mph.

In 2011, the Oakland Athletics drafted Blake and later traded him to the Washington Nationals in 2013, where he continued minor league play. In 2015, Blake was called up to the majors and in 2016 was pitching for the Nationals in the NLDS playoff game against the Los Angeles Dodgers!

Blake Treinen could have quit many times when things weren't going his way, but he continued to pursue his dream.

What have you started and put off that you would like to finish? Maybe it's finishing your college degree, or finding a career you enjoy. What do you need to do today to get started on finding your lane for success?

Finding Your Passion

In the movie *The Rookie*, Dennis Quaid plays a high school baseball coach in west Texas who had once dreamed of pitching in the major leagues. There is a scene in the movie when he is looking for some encouragement to consider trying out for a local major league team and drives to his father's house to ask for advice. His father mentions something his grandfather once said, "It's okay to think about what you want to do until it's time to start doing what you were meant to do."

What do you want to do? Answering this question can be as simple as identifying the top two or three things that are most important to you, then identifying what aligns with those values. For example, do you want autonomy to make your own schedule, or be mentored by someone you admire, or lead a team in a company? Take some time to write down your thoughts and why this is important. It's a great way to get started.

Overcoming Challenges

We all have challenges. Many times we feel stuck, like there is no way out because of where we live, being dependent on others, or certain physical challenges.

My mother Martha Ellen Thornton gave birth to me in June of 1966. I was her third child and at the age of two, the doctors discovered I had an eye tumor behind my right eye that was the size of a small potato and had become life threatening. When I think about this now as a parent, I can't imagine what my mother was feeling knowing her son would require major eye surgery while being pregnant with her fourth child. Surgery was also going to require a lot of money. My mother worked three jobs during the week just to help put food on the table for us. Despite the challenges she faced, she pushed through it with the help of family, friends, and the Edmond Lions Club, and I got the life-saving surgery I needed.

What challenges did you face growing up? Reflect on some of the lessons you learned as you overcame the challenge and use this to break through the obstacles in your way now. While it may take some support from others, you can overcome any challenge.

Don't Quit

My parents, Jack and Martha Thornton, are bowling proprietors and members of the Oklahoma City Bowling Hall of Fame for their service to the bowling community. They have both worked very hard as small business owners for more than 40 years together. This often comes with a lot of sacrifice, covering for employees when they get sick and can't make it to work, and getting up early or staying late to get everything completed.

It's a lot of responsibility to be a proprietor of a business in entertainment. I am sure there were many times when things didn't go as planned and they just felt like giving up because of the challenges of lane maintenance, making payroll, and the quality time lost with family at home.

I was fortunate to get the chance to grow up seeing some of the sacrifices involved and the perseverance my parents demonstrated as they worked through the tough times. These lessons taught me the important value of not giving up on something you start. Even when I felt like giving up on a sport, my parents told me, "You can quit playing the sport at the end of the season, but you need to finish what you signed up for."

This advice shaped my values of commitment and courage, which helped me to push through a number of obstacles in my path. I've also tried to instill the same values in my children.

Are you currently in a situation where you are pursuing the job of your dreams, or going for that big promotion in your company? Don't quit! Reach out and find others to help you get where you want to go.

Sometimes You Have to Face Your Fears

When you begin chasing your dream to get a new job or to go back to school to finish your degree, it can be stressful and even scary. This is especially true if pursuing your dreams requires a move to a new city where you don't know anyone. Now that's a challenge!

In 1984, I went off to college to attend the University of Central Oklahoma. I chose this university because I could live with my sweet grandmother, Lillian Fults, and save money on college housing. I was also familiar with the area since I had attended grade school in the same town. I remember saying goodbye to my mom and dad and then driving off with a car packed full of clothes for the next four to five months.

I loved living with my grandmother. She was always around to encourage me and support whatever I wanted to do. She enjoyed cooking breakfast and we would often have dinner in the evening. However, I was pretty nervous about college when I arrived because I didn't know anyone. But that all changed the day I went to the store to purchase a book bag.

While browsing the local sporting goods store, I met a guy, John Pellow. He invited me to his college fraternity rush party that evening. I thought this might be a good way to meet some people before class started. Later that evening I pulled into the parking area of the Alpha Tau Omega house and got out of my car. I then heard a voice shout, "You can't park there, you need to move your car!" I didn't know this person and, for whatever reason, felt so embarrassed that I got back in my car and drove away. I was in absolute fear! Not the kind of fear you feel when your life is at stake, but the kind that presses down your confidence and makes you feel unwelcomed.

Somewhere along my drive home I decided that if I was going to meet people, I needed to face the fear and turn around and go back to the event. This was one of the best decisions I made, because I was able to meet some incredible men that night, some of which are still great friends today—including John Pellow.

Have you ever been in a situation where fear took over and didn't allow you to do what you wanted to do? This is common, but when you find the right lane in life, you will find the confidence to be courageous in everything you do.

I once heard someone say, "Preparation leads to confidence, and confidence leads to courage." This is a great lesson, because when you know you are prepared, you will be able to overcome your fear with confidence and make courageous decisions that allow you to enjoy more of what life has to offer.

My good friend, Terry Forest, once shared that FEAR can also stand for "False Evidence Appearing Real." Face your fears and you will find your lane!

Make the Commitment

In 2004, I had a difficult decision to make. I was going to continue down the path of management as I had done for the previous eight years in the relocation industry, or I was going to take a leap of faith and take a position in business development. Here I am 13 years later reflecting on what it takes to have success, and the one word that comes to mind is *commitment*.

Commitment is when you say you are going to do something for a specific period, and you stay with it during easy and difficult times no matter what. As my mom used to say, "If you are going to start something, then you need to finish it!" I see this as one of the reasons for my 31 years of marriage, my 13 years working at Armstrong Relocation, and my success in volunteer organizations.

I once heard a TED Talk about getting inspired by participating in a 30-day challenge to write, or exercise, or doing something that gives you a sense of achievement upon completion. Have you ever taken a 30-day challenge and completed it? If you did, you know how great that feels.

I remember when some of my son's friends decided to do a 30-day 10,000 push-up challenge. I thought it sounded like something that would be a great achievement if successful, so I accepted the challenge.

The day it started, I was kidding my son about getting his push-ups in and he made a statement that reminded me of taking owner-ship. He said, "I'm not the one that accepted the challenge." There it was, a pivotal moment when I knew that I had to complete the challenge because *I said I would.* No excuses.

Was it difficult? Yes. Were there days when I didn't feel like completing the challenge? Yes. But I pushed through it and on day 29, I completed the 10,000th push-up. I even wrote it on a piece of paper and took a picture and posted it in the social media group.

Have you been in a situation where you felt like giving up or gave up before you reached your goal? Why are things so difficult to finish?

Many times the reason we give up on a goal is because we lose sight of the big picture and start focusing on ourselves or how we feel at the moment. The next time you set a goal for yourself, try not to focus on the difficult moments, the challenges, or the lack of progress in the short term. Remember, the long-term results are what it's all about. The journey may seem difficult at times, but the results will be worth it.

Be In It To Win It

In the spring of 2016 during my company's national sales leadership meeting, I received a badge that says "INITTOWINIT." When I see this, it reminds me of the commitments I have made to others in our company and to the clients we have built partnerships with over time. Commitment is not about being perfect, but sticking with the plan and process to achieve a goal no matter how difficult it may seem.

Are you committed to your profession, to your goals, or to your personal relationships? In other words, are you in it to win it?

My wife shared the following poem with me several years ago and I have it on my desk today. It serves as a wonderful reminder of what it means to be committed and *in it to win it.*

The Man in the Glass

When you get what you want in your struggle for self
And the world makes you king for a day
Just go to the mirror and look at yourself
And see what that man has to say.

For it isn't your father, or mother, or wife
Whose judgment upon you must pass
The fellow whose verdict counts most in your life
Is the one staring back from the glass.

He's the fellow to please — never mind all the rest
For he's with you, clear to the end
And you've passed your most difficult, dangerous test
If the man in the glass is your friend.

You may fool the whole world down the pathway of years
And get pats on the back as you pass
But your final reward will be heartache and tears
If you've cheated the man in the glass.

–Anonymous

If I Knew Then What I Know Now

My wife and I often talk about our journey. We both agree that we are more appreciative of the things we have today because we went through so many struggles early in our marriage. I have also thought about this in terms of my career. *If only I would have* . . . fill in the blank. But it's the struggles that help us grow when we take the time to learn from them.

The Christian group, MercyMe, released a hit song in 2014 from their album *Welcome to the New* called "Dear Younger Me." The song is about an older person reflecting on some of the mistakes made as a youth and how he or she would like to be able to share some of the life lessons learned to help prevent them from making the same mistakes again. The song starts like this:

> *Dear younger me*
> *Where do I start*
> *If I could tell you everything that I have learned so far*
> *Then you could be*
> *One step ahead*
> *Of all the painful memories still running thru my head*
> *I wonder how much different things would be*
> *Dear younger me*
>
> *Dear younger me*
> *I cannot decide*
> *Do I give some speech about how to get the most out of your life*
> *Or do I go deep*
> *And try to change*
> *The choices that you'll make cuz they're choices that made me*
> *Even though I love this crazy life*
> *Sometimes I wish it was a smoother ride*
> *Dear younger me, dear younger me*

Unfortunately, life is not always a smooth ride. We only get one chance on this great journey of life and cannot go back and change anything. That's why it's so important to find your lane and commit yourself to the choices you make each day. All of us have an opportunity to change the trajectory of our path by making choices to finish what we start. My hope is that today is the day you make the choice to find your lane and commit to the journey ahead you.

Chapter 1 Summary

Let's pull over and review...

It's Not How You Start, But How You Finish

Some of the most rewarding times in life will be when you finish something that is very challenging and put in a lot of hard work and sacrifice to achieve it. Is it time for you to change lanes, take a detour, or continue ahead? Consider the following questions before moving into the next chapter.

1. What's on your list that you started and always wished you had finished? Why is this important to you?

2. Do you have a defining moment? What challenges have you overcome?

3. What are some of the fears or obstacles that have prevented you from pursuing what's most important to you?

Fuel for Your Journey

Imagine how Blake Treinen would feel today if he had given up on his dream. Face your fears with courage and make the commitment to pursue what's most important to you. Take time to capture and reflect on some defining moments of your life. Write them down. If an obstacle presents itself, have the faith and courage to take whatever detour is required to get you where you want to go.

Remember—it's not how you start, but how you finish!

> *"Ask yourself 3 times a day what's important to you, then have the courage to build your life around your answer."*
>
> **–Tom Watson**

THE ROUTE YOU CHOOSE MATTERS

"The true test of a man's character is what he does when no one is watching."

–John Wooden

Have you ever made the wrong choice? Sometimes this is how we learn. However, when you have a pattern of bad choices, it will often lead you down a difficult road and put you in the wrong lane, making life very challenging.

Your Choices Will Shape You

I grew up in a small town. Great times walking with friends to lunch, driving our cars on the weekends as teenagers, and lots of other fun activities. In high school, I enjoyed playing both football and baseball. We had some great teams and memorable moments, one of which included playing in a state baseball championship.

Some of your most memorable moments aren't going to be the games but the journey along the way. For me those moments were the bus rides with the team and playing card games like poker and spades, with the boom box blasting the songs of the '80s.

Friends can influence the choices you make. But in the end, *you* are the one making the choice. I have been fortunate to be surrounded by great friends on this journey in life, but I also know some of the dumbest choices I've made in life were when I was surrounded by people who were living for the moment with little concern for the impact it had on others. Let me share one of those examples.

I was hanging around some friends one night who decided to climb the tallest building in town, which was the bank building on Main Street. This building was the center point of the main drag for people cruising around the town. A few of us guys climbed the small building in the back alley down the street, then worked our way up to the top deck of the bank building and peaked over to see down below. It was really high at the time. We were all laughing and hanging out until we saw flashlights and heard a voice say, "What are you boys doing up here?" It was the police, and we were in big trouble.

When I look back I think about how dumb that really was for me to do. We could have slipped and fell, or even been shot had we been mistaken for bank robbers.

A Tale of Two Choices

I was recently reflecting on my daughter's college selection process and it reminded me how closely aligned it is with trying to select a company to work for, or when a manager is considering an employee for a promotion. It's all about perception.

Several years ago after her high school graduation, our daughter decided to visit two universities for her college education. She was planning to major in nutritional science and was excited about the journey ahead. So she set up a tour with two colleges, both of which were major universities. I was fascinated by the difference between each college visit.

When we visited the first college, it was a beautiful day. The sun was shining and the weather was about 75 degrees. It was amazing! We went in to register for the orientation and found our group for the tour. The tour guide was a student at the university. He was smiling, upbeat, positive, and passionate about his school. As we walked around, he shared his stories about the different areas on campus that he enjoyed from the student union to the rec center to game days. He was engaging and connected with his group during the tour. He was proud of his school and transferred these feelings to students taking the tour. When we left, my daughter was feeling pretty good about the college but said she was going to keep her options open as she still had another college to tour before she made a decision.

When we went to visit the second college, it was a cool morning and overcast with impending rain. We went to the orientation meeting, and then met with our group for the campus tour. The tour guide was also a student, but this guide was much different than the first. He was not very engaging and didn't really have much energy. When asked about certain areas, he didn't really engage with the group other than share what each place was, not the experience. When we walked by the football field, we thought it might be cool to check it out, but he said it was off limits. I thought he missed a great opportunity to share game day stories, or something to let others know what it would be like as a student. By the end of the tour, my daughter turned to me and said she didn't need to think about it— she had made her decision to attend the first college we visited.

So what made the difference? Perception!

Both universities were great places to get a college education, but the tour guide that was positive and shared experiences that helped others to feel what it would be like to be part of the journey made the difference.

It doesn't matter if you are a college student or work in customer service, operations, HR, or payroll. Positive, passionate people that are able to connect, ask questions, and build relationships will get the promotion every time.

Are you the tour guide for college #1 or #2? Ask someone you know for feedback to see what changes you can make to create a positive perception in others. It could lead to your next big promotion!

Know Your Strengths

Have you ever been asked what your strengths are and not really been able to provide clarity in your answer? When you are unsure, it might mean you are driving in the wrong lane and you need to get back on track.

In 1995, my wife and I decided to pack up and move our family to Dallas, Texas to start new careers. I joined a relocation company in Dallas called Daryl Flood Warehouse and Movers. This company had a philosophy that if you work in sales or management, you need to start from the ground up, which meant spending some time on the trucks to gain operational experience. So I packed boxes, moved furniture, and worked in the warehouse that summer learning the business.

During that time I was approached by the general manager and asked if my strength was more sales or operations. I thought about how I received my degree in business administration with a focus on management. At the same time, I also knew I had good people skills. So I told him I was pretty balanced, which kept me on the management track in operations.

I really didn't know what to say at the time. I didn't know what my strength was at all. It really bothered me, because I didn't really know my purpose at the time—I was just trying to make enough money to raise my family.

I worked there as a manager for several years before making a change to lead another small company as the general manager. However, there were a few times I remember feeling more passionate about my job than others. It was when I was involved with intentional leadership growth sessions and around the sales process. It was invigorating to find a solution for the customer and to feel like I was able to help families during a stressful time. I wasn't sure where I was headed, but knew I needed to take a different route to experience more joy in my life.

In 2004, I joined Armstrong Relocation in Dallas in a sales role. Since then I have enjoyed tremendous success over the years and haven't looked back.

A large part of my success as a leader is due to finding the courage necessary to leverage my strengths of connecting with people and creating strategic partnerships to help others in business and in the community.

What is your strength? Are you in the lane you want to be in right now or do you need to find the courage to try something different for success? Understanding and drawing upon your strengths may be just what you need to find your lane.

Choose to Learn About Yourself

One of the things you can do to find out more about yourself is to take a self-assessment. There are many self-assessments available online. You can also learn more about yourself by observing other leaders.

I once had an epiphany when our leadership team was taking a self-assessment as a group with other leaders in the company. One of the exercises was to circle the top 5 values out of 30 or 40 and rank them 1 to 5, with 1 being the most important. Though I don't remember which ones were important to me at the time, what I do remember is when the facilitator took a poll for each value. It seemed like there were a few hands that went up for each value, but when the value of integrity came up, I observed something that has stuck with me since that day. Not a few, but *everyone* on the senior executive leadership team, including the CEO, raised their hand when asked about integrity as being the most important value.

I recognized the importance of the value of integrity as a leader back then, but that day I realized how important this value was to me personally. It was a learning moment for me as I observed other leaders' perspectives.

What have you observed in other leaders? So much can be learned from talking to other leaders and watching how they approach situations. This is why it's important as a leader to always do the right thing—you never know who might be watching.

Choose to Add Value

Have you ever heard of the 80/20 rule? Often I hear in volunteer organizations, that 20% of the people do 80% of the work, or 20% of customers provide 80% of the revenue. This theory can be aligned with many different scenarios.

I always wonder why people sign up to be a volunteer and don't really try to add any value. They are there along for the ride. Do you know anyone like this?

Adding value is a choice. When you find your lane, you can't help but choose to add value to others.

When I was 12 years old, I signed up to walk in the March of Dimes Walk-a-Thon. This organization exists to improve the health of babies by preventing birth defects, premature birth, and infant mortality. The walk is an opportunity to raise money by asking people you know to sponsor you per mile for donations. The 20-mile walk was from our home town to the lake about 10 miles outside of town, then back to the finish line. It was a blast! There were some people that ran it very fast, while others walked it slowly, and many did not finish. However, I was going to finish because I was going for the most donations.

You see, the most donations won the big prize each year. I had a great audience to get donations with my parents owning a bowling center, but I still had to do the work. Every night during league bowling, I would walk up and down the center to ask for donations. Some people smiled and said no thanks, while others cheerfully sponsored me anywhere from 5 cents to $1.00 per mile.

I have several takeaways from this experience. One, when you say you are going to do something, you really need to be committed to finish what you started. Second, when you make the choice to add value, you create consistency, trust, and credibility. You believe in what you are doing and create value by sharing your perspective.

What value can you add to the people in your network?

Asking for Feedback is a Choice

Asking for feedback is one of the best things you can do to evaluate your leadership growth. Everyone sees things differently, and each different perspective can provide direction and alignment to help you find the lane that works best for you.

In 2002, I enrolled in the Dale Carnegie leadership course. This training required a huge commitment over an eight-week period. Dale Carnegie was the author of *How to Win Friends and Influence People*. His book was first published in 1936 and is still on the New York Times' best seller list 80 years later. Some of the takeaways include the importance of remembering a person's a name because "… a person's name is to that person the sweetest and most important sound in any language," and "You can make more friends in two months by becoming interested in other people than you can in two years by trying to get other people interested in you." It is a game changer for relationship building!

One of the activities we would do at the end of each session was give feedback to each other. This was priceless! This gave me great insight for improvement in my daily life. One of the best things anyone can do is to evaluate your growth as a leader. A great strategy is to reach out to close business partners and friends and ask them the following three questions:

What should I start doing?

What should I stop doing?

What should I continue doing?

Asking for feedback can be very beneficial and can also build great confidence, but you have to be ready to act and not take it personal.

Strengthfinders 2.0 is also a great book to consider purchasing. The book purchase includes a code that allows you access to an online personal assessment. This assessment includes a number of timed questions that require you to respond with your first instinct. At the end of the assessment, you are provided with your top 5 leadership traits as well as a defined assessment about each trait. You can go through the book and confirm each meaning and how you might match up with someone with other traits. There are lots of other assessments you can also take, including the DISC behavioral assessment, which is offered by many HR professionals.

The point is that you need to always be evaluating yourself for progress, and look at your progress through different perspectives. Feedback and self-assessments can often help you see your blind spots and shape you into a better leader.

Have you taken a self-assessment lately? Did the results align with your values? What can you do now to find your lane for success?

Make the Choice to Make Every Day Matter

One of the founders of Armstrong Relocation is Jim Watson. He once said, "Every day is a good day and some days are even better." This is especially true when we find our lane. The choice to have a good day and approach to life is up to you.

Many times you might feel like you are on an island and unable to gain any momentum. This is okay. We all feel like this once in a while. The important thing is to focus on the things that matter each day and invest in these things with a positive attitude. Everything else will take care of itself.

In John Maxwell's book *Today Matters: 12 Daily Practices to Guarantee Tomorrow's Success*, he shares some important principles that I have tried to incorporate into my life. I carry a modified version of these practices in my wallet and often send a copy to people when sharing a personal note with them. It reminds me of the things that matter to me and what's important to focus on each day.

TODAY MATTERS

12 Daily Practices to Guarantee Tomorrow's Success

1. ATTITUDE...gives me possibilities.
2. PRIORITIES...give me focus.
3. HEALTH...gives me strength.
4. FAMILY...gives me stability.
5. THINKING...gives me an advantage.
6. COMMITMENT...gives me tenacity.
7. FINANCES...give me options.
8. FAITH...gives me peace.
9. RELATIONSHIPS...give me fulfillment.
10. GENEROSITY...gives me significance.
11. VALUES...give me direction.
12. GROWTH...gives me potential.

Chapter 2 Summary

Let's pull over and review...

The Route You Choose Matters

Is it time to make different choices based on your beliefs, or continue down the same path? Some of the questions you might consider before moving into the next chapter include:

1. Do the choices you make align with who you want to be? What beliefs and values matter to you when making decisions to pursue your dreams?

2. Do you find yourself looking back wishing you had made different choices? Write down those events and how they made you feel.

3. What choices can you make today to get you looking and moving forward on your journey?

Fuel for Your Journey

When choosing your route, make sure to include self-awareness because the choices you make will make you. Consider taking a self-awareness test and asking others close to you for feedback. Observing other successful people will help you understand their perspective and inspire you to make choices that align with your beliefs. When you choose this route, you will find the lane that helps you grow.

> *"In matters of style, swim with the current. In matters of principle, stand like a rock."*
>
> **–Thomas Jefferson**

SET YOUR WHEELS IN MOTION

"Your actions are so loud I can't hear you."

–Ralph Waldo Emerson

H ave you ever wished you had a different schedule, could take a vacation, or do something different to get out of a slump? Many people dream about a lot of things, but never take action.

Taking Action is the Beginning

In 2004, I was thinking about making a career change. I wasn't really motivated in my leadership position and was stuck wondering what I could do to experience more joy in my career. I wasn't really doing much about it either, other than thinking about how I wished things were different.

One morning when my wife and I were attending church, a young man stood up to share his journey of faith. One of the things that struck me was when he talked about a book he read by John Ortberg, *If You Want to Walk on Water, You've Got to Get Out of the Boat.*

I remember thinking God was talking directly to me that Sunday morning. I reflected about this moment over the next day and went to purchase the book to explore what it was all about. Life is full of defining moments and this was one of them for me. It was time to take a step of faith and get out of the boat to take action in my life.

Have you ever found yourself sitting idly by or spinning your wheels? Now is the time to take action. One way to get started is to ask questions of people close to you and open yourself to their perspectives. Accepting the status quo isn't helping you or the company you work for.

Taking Action Includes Taking Risks

There was a point in my life when I decided to take action and start interviewing with companies to find a different route for success. I had received a couple of different job offers and needed to make a decision on the lane that was going to be best for me.

One of the offers was doing the same thing as a manager leading a team. This was a great opportunity with excellent salary, but I was in my late 30s and looking for something new and exciting to do in my life. However, I was really excited about another offer, which was a national account sales position that would offer me a new start, but it included a whopping 50% pay cut with potential commissions—if successful. This was a tough choice because it meant taking a risk and getting out of my comfort zone if I decided to take the sales position.

In 2016, I celebrated 12 years as a sales professional and will say it was the best choice I have ever made in my career. I wouldn't be sharing some of the leadership strategies in this book if it weren't for getting out of the boat that day and taking a risk.

Have you been in a situation where you thought about doing something different, but didn't take action because you were comfortable? The next thing you know you are looking back wondering what it might have been like. Change requires action! Connecting with people who can serve as guides can also be of benefit.

Before making my decision, I reached out and spoke with people in sales, I spoke with my mentors, and I discussed it with my family. You don't have to do this alone. You just have to take action, and then be committed to the decision.

Taking Chances Can Bring You the Most Joy

Several years ago I attended a conference in Chicago and got to hear Mike Singletary, NFL Hall of Fame player for the Chicago Bears, speak during the closing session. Mike shared several inspiring stories about his family life and football career. There was lots of laughter and sadness throughout his message. However, there was one takeaway that has impacted my life for the last 15 years.

Mike shared that throughout his football career, from high school to professional football, people would say that he couldn't do things—when in his mind he knew he could if he worked hard enough. His determination and hard work helped him find a way around all the "no's" in his life.

When he was a rookie for the bears, Mike shared a story that he was only supposed to be on kickoffs because he needed to learn the defense as a rookie. Mike said that he was anxious and ready to play defense and was trying to find a way to get in. On one play, a defensive player got hurt and the coach turned to another linebacker to go in, but he pointed and said Mike is already on the field. Well, the rest is history as Mike became a Hall of Fame linebacker, which included a Super Bowl championship.

I love that story!

Has someone ever told you that you couldn't do something before? You can do anything you want to do if you are willing to put in the work for it.

At that same conference, each attendee had a different color sticker because there were over a thousand people in attendance. The facilitator advised that if you had a blue sticker, you could enter a special room to meet Mike and get an autograph. My heart broke when I looked down to see that I didn't have a blue sticker. I began to think about how Mike had been told he "can't" his whole life and set out to find a way. I stood out in the hall for about 30 minutes watching the people with blue stickers enter a room to meet Mike Singletary. I was determined to get in that room.

After about an hour the line dwindled to about 10 people and I saw an opportunity to get inside the room. It was now or never! I went for it and slipped into the back of the line. A few minutes later, I was standing next to Mike Singletary and sharing how much his message inspired me.

Why not use this approach when you are making a move? When someone tells you no or you can't, don't give up—find a way! When you find a way to do something others told you wasn't possible, you will be inspired to pursue your dreams.

If at First You Don't Succeed, Try Again

Just because you fail doesn't mean you won't succeed later on or with another opportunity. A close friend of mine, Phil Byers, once shared a Miami Herald newspaper clipping about some very famous people that failed many times during their career. Think about what would have happened if the people below would have quit after failing at something:

- Henry Ford forgot to put reverse on his first automobile.
- Thomas Edison invented the perpetual cigar and cement furniture before coming up with the light bulb.
- Albert Einstein's parents were told he was mentally retarded.
- Michael Jordan was cut from his high school basketball team.
- Elvis Presley didn't make the glee club.
- Napoleon finished near the bottom of his military school class.
- Abraham Lincoln failed many times in politics before becoming President.
- The Beetles were turned down by a recording contract from Decca Records.
- Steven Spielberg dropped out of high school and hung around movie studios shooting 8mm film.
- John Grisham's first novel was rejected by agents and publishers.

- Babe Ruth struck out 1,330 times, which was a major league record at the time.

It's okay to make mistakes. This is how you learn and grow. If you really want to do something great, you have to be willing to make a few mistakes and learn from them along the way. As you can see, Babe Ruth struck out over 1000 times, but he became known for hitting home runs as a professional baseball player.

Taking Action Means Making Mistakes

My mother's favorite saying is "no biggie." If you made a mistake or didn't get the results you were looking for, she would smile and say, "It's no biggie," which meant no big deal, go try again until you find success or the outcome you are looking for.

We often think about things or dream big dreams but never take the steps to put them into action. I remember being like this in several phases of my life before finding my lane. I also have seen this in others and try coaching them or offering words of encouragement, because I know they have incredible talent and just need to take the steps to make things happen.

My youngest son recently graduated from college and was ready to step out in the world in his new career. Dana and I tried to encourage him to send out his resume and reach out to different companies to help him get some experience. But because he had been so focused on school, he wanted to take some time out to just think about what he wanted to do and get mentally prepared. I thought this was okay since he still had the job he had when he started college, and he made his own car and insurance payments while living at home. So I waited about three months before engaging him in conversations about the importance of getting started and taking action.

If you're finding it difficult to get started, one of the things you can do to create momentum is to begin a 21-day challenge. Such a challenge is designed around action items that are to be completed every day for 21 days. You can do this for anything you want to improve about yourself or in your life. Each day can include research (preparation), connecting with others, and taking daily action steps. It's not so much about the end goal, but more about the process of creating momentum.

Have you ever been in a slump or thought about making improvements but didn't take any action? I have heard this referred to as "paralysis by analysis," which means there's too much thinking and not enough doing. This is your time to start writing down some ways to help you set your wheels in motion.

Taking Action Means Not Looking Back

Once you decide to get out of your comfort zone, it will get tough, and when tough times are upon you, you have to push through the process and not look back. This is the time you need to remember why you decided to pursue a different route. Don't be one of those people who can't get past their past.

We have all made bad choices at one time or another in our life, but the best way to get past this is to start thinking about who you are today and how each past lesson shaped your life for the better. Think about it—you wouldn't be the same person today if you wouldn't have made some of those choices and learned from them.

Years ago I was asked to speak on the topic of relocation along with other speakers during some breakout sessions at a small conference in Dallas. There were about 100 people at the conference and 6 breakout sessions following the general session. Once the keynote speaker ended, all the attendees got up to go to the breakout session of their choice. I had prepared for this presentation for the last week and was looking forward to sharing with others. I was expecting about 15 attendees (hoping for more) based on the attendance, and when all the doors closed I only saw two people sitting in the room. Gulp!

Now, I could have said, "We don't have enough people for our presentation and you can go to another session," but instead I focused on the people that showed up. I was appreciative of the opportunity to share strategies with the people that wanted to attend my session.

This story reminds me of an interview with country music singer Charlie Daniels, well known for his hit song "The Devil Went Down to Georgia." When asked what advice he would give young singers coming up in the business, he said, "Don't ever look at the empty seats."

This is true in business and in your personal life. Add value to the people that are in your people zone. Don't worry about who is not there, but on the gratitude of the people around you in the moment.

Don't Give Up

My boss once shared a story about a guy that was digging for gold. He found traces of ore to give him hope to continue digging. At first things started well for the gold digger, but the trail disappeared shortly after he started digging. The man continued to dig trying to find the gold, but found nothing. After a while, he quit with frustration and sold his machinery to a junk man for a few hundred dollars. After he went home in disappointment, the wise junk man called in a mining engineer who checked the mine and calculated that there was a vein of gold just three feet from where the man had stopped digging. The junk man went on to make millions of dollars from the gold mine.

The lesson to be learned from that story is that in order to be successful, you need to stay focused on the mission and persevere through difficult times.

The next time you feel like giving up on your dream, remember you might just be three feet from gold!

Chapter 3 Summary

Let's pull over and review...

Set Your Wheels in Motion

Have you dreamed of doing something different, more meaningful but have not taken any action to get started? Many times it takes courage and willingness to take a detour or exit to find the best lane for you. Some of the questions you might consider before moving into the next chapter include:

1. What are some of the things that are holding you back from pursuing your dreams?

2. What actions do you need to take to pursue your dreams?

3. What is one thing you can do today to move you closer to achieving your goals?

Fuel for Your Journey

Setting your wheels in motion means shifting from park to drive and moving forward with your goals. Remember, the art is in the start! If you want to do something different, write it down and then share it with others to get their perspective for feedback. You will feel a fire ignite in you that will give you energy and excitement.

It may take you a few tries to find your lane, and you may have some setbacks along the way. When you do, just say to yourself, "It's no biggie," and keep driving!

> *"There are three types of people in this world: those who make things happen, those who watch things happen, and those who wonder what happened."*
>
> **—Mary Kay Ash**

PLANNING—YOUR MAP TO SUCCESS

*"What you get by achieving your goals is not as important as
what you become by achieving your goals."*

–Zig Ziglar

Making a job change or deciding to go back to school can be challenging. We have all made job changes or thought about doing something different. One of the most important things you can do when thinking about making a change is to develop a written plan.

Planning is the Key

When I received an opportunity to interview with Armstrong Relocation, I decided to make a plan as if I had the job and was already working. During my interview, I shared this plan and how I would carry it out if I were hired.

I had not been in this position before and understood the risk associated with failing in this profession. I also knew that I wouldn't be able to start out with a high salary since I didn't have any current business. However, I knew with a good plan, I'd have a compass and guide to keep me focused and on task to achieve my plan.

Taking the time to create that plan paid off. Not only did I get hired, during my first year I was able to land a couple of prospects on my list, and five years later I lead our company in sales in my market.

Leaders want to know that you have a plan and are committed to the plan when they are considering you for a new position. Even if you are already in a role, it's important to set aside time each year to establish goals and a plan to help you succeed as a leader.

Lack of Planning

Have you ever gone to the grocery store without a list and got home only to realize you forget one of the things you needed most? We've all been there!

In 2002, I had just taken on a new leadership role in Dallas for a relocation company called The Federal Companies, an agent for Allied Van Lines, and was trying to make my mark as a young operations leader. I was hired to elevate our quality and culture by hiring, training, and inspiring our team. It seemed like a 24/7 job at the time, but I was committed to the goal of growing the company. I was also responsible for facilities that were in poor condition at the time.

At times, I really felt like I was in over my head, but the more great people I hired, the easier it was to lead the team. I enjoyed a lot of success during that time, but also made a lot of mistakes along the way. There was one mistake that has stuck with me for years, but made me a better leader today.

Our parking lot was awful. It was filled with lots of potholes and it not only looked bad, but was not good for our employees' and guests' vehicles to drive on each day. It was rather embarrassing and on my list of improvements.

One day, a gentleman came into my office and told me he had been working down the road and had additional asphalt to fill in the potholes of our parking lot. I thought it was a great idea so I let my leadership team know that I would be out of the office the following Friday, but there would be some guys filling the potholes while I was gone.

I arrived at the office on Saturday morning and was surprised to see a BRAND NEW PARKING LOT with fresh yellow stripes! It looked wonderful, but I was in shock because I knew that it surely cost more than filling some of the potholes like we agreed.

I called the guy and he informed me that one of our leaders mentioned to go ahead and finish the parking lot since they had extra asphalt. When I told him our price agreement, he quickly pointed out that the price quoted in the document I signed was PER SQUARE FOOT. Needless to say, the new parking lot was a far greater expense than filling a few potholes. YIKES!

I would have been in a much better position if I would have properly planned the parking lot project. I could have done my research and asked others in my network for advice. I could have also collaborated with other team members instead of trying to do everything on my own. In this case, we worked out a final cost agreement. However, it was very stressful during the process only because I had not invested in a good plan.

You learn so much when you fail. I often hear leaders say to fail early and fail often—it's the fastest way to success.

The thing we can learn from failing is the importance of owning it and learning from it. People will accept your mistakes as a part of learning as long as you own your failures and respond quickly to show that you understand what happened and how to prevent it from happening again.

Kevin O'Leary of the TV series, Shark Tank, once said, "The road to success is filled with potholes of failure." This is something you have to be willing to accept and own when you make mistakes.

Planning Takes Time

We all have our list of daily activities that we try to accomplish. Many of us write down the things we need to get completed on a to-do list each day or week. This helps us focus on completing the things that matter most. Most days we try to do all we can, but at the end of the day there just doesn't seem to be enough time.

So what is the best approach to achieving one's action items each day?

I have asked this question over and over throughout my career and tried to figure out who has the best approach. One thing I found was a lot of similarities, and common threads, but in the end it's about finding your lane and what works best for you.

For example, I know one top business leader that schedules 15 minutes at the end of each work day to review the following day and list his top action items so that he is ready to go when he wakes up the next day. I tried this approach for a little while, and it just didn't work for me on a consistent basis. The key here is consistency! There would be times it worked great, then other times I was in the middle of a project and was trying to get out of the office in order to make my next appointment, and I would skip writing down my items.

I also interviewed a top leader that said he reviews his action items 30 minutes before he goes to bed each evening so that he is ready to go the next day. This is a great approach to consider instilling into your daily discipline. You can do this at the end of the work day, before you go to bed, or when you wake up in the morning.

As for me, I like making a list of action items at the start of the week and plugging the most important items into my calendar to make sure they get completed.

It doesn't matter which system you have as long as you have a system to be productive. However, there is one area that many people miss when planning.

I was recently having a conversation with a business partner when she mentioned that she had some big strategic goals, but was so caught up in daily tasks she couldn't seem to get a grip on getting started. This is a common problem and challenge for many business professionals, coaches, teachers, and parents. A way around this is to identify your long-term goals and then break them down into short-term goals. This will remove the stress of being overwhelmed and help keep you on track during the process as you achieve milestones along the way. Don't forget to include others!

One of the things I do at the end of each year is write down a list of things I want to accomplish the following year in both my business and personal life. I even give it a theme like 15 in 2015! This is a great time to dream about what this achievement will look like and to have some fun sharing with others. The most important thing is to identify the top three goals that will make the most impact. This is where strategy takes over.

Let's say you are an HR leader and you want to accomplish a leadership development program in the next 6 to 12 months. You are probably not putting this on your daily action item list because you have more pressing issues. However, if you make this one of your top three goals, it will be in the front of your mind to ask questions of others and to schedule small amounts of time to work on your plan.

The key is to ensure the decisions and choices you make during the year align with your top three goals for the year. This will help you focus on the most important things you want to accomplish at year-end. Just as important is scheduling time on your calendar to work on your goals. It's amazing what happens when things get scheduled.

Earlier this summer my wife mentioned that since her summer break was starting, we should schedule a vacation before the summer was over. Due to my work schedule, I have all of my meetings listed in my calendar and mentioned that we needed to sync our calendars and discuss some dates that might work for the both of us. When we reviewed our calendars, we started writing down things that we wanted to do like drive to our parents' home in Oklahoma for the weekend, and take a vacation to Angel Fire, New Mexico. We had something scheduled for most weekends, and the couple of weekends that weren't scheduled we planned to just relax and get some things done around the house. So we planned our vacation!

At the end of the summer, we felt like we enjoyed a great summer and accomplished a lot together. This is because we intentionally wrote down the things that were important to us and took the time to schedule those things on our calendars.

Successful business leaders and coaches always know their top priority items. It's about focusing on the items that will make the most impact in your business and your personal life. Yes, you need to have your daily list of action items, but they also need to align with your top three goals.

I once heard Darren Hardy call this your BHAGs—Big Hairy Audacious Goals. Maybe you write them down on a white board so others can see them when you walk into the office. I actually put an easel in my office and update it each quarter so that when other teammates come into my office, they can see where I'm spending my time and what I'm focused on. Many times it drives great conversation.

If you accomplish one of your goals before the year ends, then replace it with another so that you always have eyes on the target and keep the needle moving for you and your team. Trying various strategies will also help you find the lane that works best for you.

When Things Don't Go as Planned

One of the best parts about leadership growth is investing time to reflect on your past and identifying leadership lessons to share with others. In the early '90s, I was meeting my wife at the local car dealership to check on getting her automobile serviced. My 4-year-old son was sitting in the passenger seat of my truck, and my 2-year-old daughter was strapped into her car seat in the middle next to me. After a few minutes, I put my truck in park and got out to see how things were going. Suddenly, my wife shouted, "Your truck is moving!"

I immediately ran to the truck, opened the door, put my foot on the brake, and then shifted my truck into park—right after it rammed into a brand new car. When I looked over, I saw that my daughter had found a way to get out of her car seat and lean on the steering wheel and gear shift, which put my truck in drive. Looking at my son, I said, "Why did you let her do this?" He looked at me with his straight face and said, "Dad, I didn't know she could drive!" I smiled and immediately knew one thing was true—I needed to take responsibility for this accident, because I didn't turn off the vehicle when I made the decision to get out of the truck.

Many times we don't think about the importance of *responsibility*, which is a relative to the word *accountability*. When you say you are going to do something, are you committed no matter what gets in the way? How about goal setting and follow-up? When you fail, do you think about whose fault it was, or do you look for the gaps to close when you face a similar situation in the future?

I once heard Robin Roberts say that her mom would always tell her to "make her mess her message." Taking responsibility is critical to moving forward in your leadership growth.

Hold Yourself Accountable to the Plan

De La Salle High School, in Concord, California, was recently featured in the movie *When the Game Stands Tall*, featuring head football coach Bob Ladouceur's teams, which won 151 consecutive high school football games from 1992 to 2004—a winning streak that stands today.

One of my favorite parts of the movie (and most impacting) is how the team prepared for the season during practice. Each player wrote down his commitment for the week on a small index card and shared it with another player. The other player would say that he accepted the commitment and they'd shake hands. Talk about POWERFUL!

What if we all shared a commitment with our colleagues each week in business? It might be a commitment to getting reports in on time, returning all customer calls within a certain time period, or commitment to spending 30 minutes with a different employee each week to learn more about their story and how you might better support them.

When you prepare and hold each other accountable, you can accomplish things that you didn't think would be possible. It may be preparing for a job interview, or a sales presentation, or teaching a class. When you plan, you have a compass to guide you along the way.

Dream Big When Planning Excellence

Excellence doesn't just happen. It starts with a plan for execution. When I decided to take the sales position with Armstrong, I wasn't looking for just another job. I was looking for an opportunity to have autonomy and grow into being a business leader to add value for others in the company. When I started in my role, I quickly made a one-year, three-year and five-year plan and set big goals to achieve.

Once you achieve a goal, it's important to think ahead to your next goal. I always go back to what Lou Holtz said when it came to what he feared most as a football coach—"the perils of being #1." It is vital to continue setting new goals for continued growth. It starts with a vision about something you truly believe in that will make impact when you achieve the vision.

Here are five things you might consider doing to stay connected to your plan for maximum success:

1. Write it down.
2. Share with your inner circle.
3. Review progress.
4. Celebrate success.
5. Set new goals.

The above plan can help navigate you like a compass and help guide you through the process of success. I often hear great coaches talking about how the most important thing in football for players is going through "the process." It probably won't happen overnight. At least it didn't for me! It often takes weeks, months, and even years to achieve success, but it starts with a vision and a plan to strive for, one that keeps you in alignment with your daily choices. It also takes discipline to make the choices you need to make each day.

Once you set a goal and begin the process, you'll find each day will not be glamorous. There will be challenging and difficult times that cause you frustration and sometimes even depression when you feel like you aren't getting anywhere. Just remember this is part of the process. Enjoy the small wins and the many lessons learned along the way—they will help pave the way to greatness. Look to them as your guide and compass!

Have you ever started driving to an unfamiliar address in a major city without a GPS or map? This is what it would be like when you don't plan for execution in business. You would have little confidence in your ability to find your way and experience a great deal of stress along the way.

Start with a plan and you will achieve some amazing success in your life. The best part is when you find your lane—it's the most amazing experience ever!

Now, take some time to think about what you want to achieve and write it down and share it with some of the people in your network for feedback and accountability. Be sure to think big, then go get started on your new adventure!

Chapter 4 Summary

Let's pull over and review…

PLANNING—Your Map to Success

Have you ever reached out to someone you know and asked them about their daily planning or daily disciplines? Now is the time! You may not need to copy what works for them, but you might find some inspiration in their methods and daily disciplines to incorporate into your planning strategies. Some of the tasks/questions to consider before moving to the next chapter include:

1. Do you have a plan? What are some things you would like to accomplish over the next year? How about the next 5 to 10 years?

2. Do you invest personal time during the year to think about the future? What are your top three goals?

3. How can you hold yourself more accountable to your plan?

Fuel for Your Journey

Planning is your map to success. Use it to guide you as you plan your weekly schedule (don't forget to put each task in your calendar) and you will see how much easier it is to get results. Print out your goals and share them with someone this week so they can help hold you accountable for achievement. Share your map with others for the best chance at success!

> *"The only ones you try to get even with are the ones that do you good."*
>
> **–Lillian V. Fults**

THE CARPOOL LANE

"I'm not the smartest fellow in the world, but I sure can pick smart colleagues."

–Franklin D. Roosevelt

I was in the 7th grade attending Northwood Middle School in the fall of 1978 when I was impacted by an amazing teacher named Gilman (Gil) Davis. Toward the end of our class period, Mr. Davis was sharing information and teaching us about student council and volunteer responsibilities as a leader. I was listening to his words very closely because I was running for class president. When someone in the classroom asked who students should vote for, I listened even more closely and followed his instructions. Those instructions have helped me for more than 30 years. Here is the wisdom he shared: "Vote for the person that looks you in the eye, shakes your hand, and asks how he can help you."

So you know what I did the rest of the week before school, at lunch, during recess, and after school? That's right—I shook every student's hand in school and asked how I could help them. A few weeks later my name was announced as the 7th grade class president.

Start Developing Your Network

What I realize today is that Mr. Davis was teaching his students about leadership, networking, AND how to add value to others. It's important to be a good listener and understand other people's perspective so you can add value when growing your network.

Tom Izzo, coach of Michigan State, coined the phrase "Learn to listen and listen to learn." Developing your network allows you and others to be resourceful.

When developing your network, look for the encouragers and those that share your beliefs. Being around like-minded people will increase your confidence and inspire you to pursue your dreams and take action for success.

You may have heard the adage "Your network is your net worth." There is nothing more valuable than the value of a network among your family, friends, business partners, and community.

Do you have a network of business partners or friends that add value to each other?

Next time you meet someone new, find a way to connect so that you can be a resource to help them achieve their goals and dreams. It might be sharing an article or just sending an encouraging note. Who knows, one day they might share how you lifted them to success. When you choose this route, success will surely follow.

Send Personal Letters to Add Value to Your Network

Sending personal written notes by mail isn't as common today as it was years ago. Today, we have so many ways of communicating such as texting on our cell phones, sending an email, and a multitude of social media communication channels. However, not too many things are more powerful than sending/receiving a personal note in the mail.

I have enjoyed sending and receiving notes for many years. It's amazing what a personal encouraging note or card will do to lift your spirits. I was also inspired when I learned that George W. Bush's dad also shared this passion. After reading the book *41: A Portrait of My Father*, by George W. Bush, I sent a personal note to the President letting him know how much I enjoyed the book. A few months later I received a personal note from him. Now that was pretty special!

One of my favorite letters was a note I received around 2009 from Dave Nelson, Vice President of Sales at Armstrong Relocation. He sent me a copy of the United Van Lines Convention program attached with a personal note written to me that said he was looking forward to seeing me there one day as a "Presidents Club nominee." This was inspiring and put hope in my path knowing someone was out there cheering for me along the ups and downs of sales. Fortunately, I was able to share this story with our team in 2014 when I was added to the "Presidents Club" for the first time at the convention.

Unfortunately, when we communicate by way of social media and email, it is hard to capture some of these uplifting notes for our kids and grandkids to read in the future. There can be so much joy when reading a letter from your grandmother or grandfather.

In George W. Bush's book, he shares many of the notes his father wrote to his family and friends throughout his life. His approach to sharing life lessons can be so encouraging. It is so inspiring to see how he shared his thoughts to help others. My hope is for all of us to be more disciplined to make this a priority when opportunity presents itself.

Take an opportunity this week to write a personal note to someone on your mind that you can encourage, or just to let them know you are thinking about them. It will make a difference!

Take the First Step

When you go to an event, do you look for someone you know or stand around waiting for people to introduce themselves to you? It's amazing what happens when you meet someone and learn about where they work or where they live. But sometimes you have to take the first step. For example, George H.W. Bush had a rule of thumb to introduce himself when he was within 10 feet of someone he didn't know.

When I was in middle school running for student council president, my history teacher encouraged kids to vote for the person that took that first step to shake their hand. Everyone has a story they want to share, but someone has to take the first step to initiate the conversation—make that someone YOU.

I have learned so much from the people that I have included on my journey. In relocation, I have met customers, business partners, CEO's, HR leaders and so many others that have helped shape my career. This aligns so much with a saying by Jim Rohn, a famous author and speaker in the subject of personal development: "The person you will be in 5 years is based on the books you read and the people you surround yourself with today."

A great business network or circle of friends will not only help provide good direction for you to make good choices, but will also provide access to people that will open more doors for you to be your very best.

Next time you are at an event, find the courage to take the first step and go up and introduce yourself. It can be a game changer for both of you.

Volunteer to Grow Your Network

Do you volunteer? There are so many organizations looking for volunteers these days including non-profit industry associations, community service organizations, and more.

I have volunteered nearly all of my life. It's because I like to make a difference while getting to know other people. I'm sure you are the same way. Volunteering is a great way to meet people, expand your network, and learn leadership skills along the way.

When I was in grade school, I volunteered to help raise money for the March of Dimes walk-a-thon. When I was in junior high, I volunteered for student council. When I was working with my father in his business, I volunteered for an industry organization called the

Southwest Bowling Proprietors Association Board of Directors (thanks to my father paving the way for me). I volunteered to coach my children's sports teams and served on several community boards. Today I continue to serve on leadership boards, which include DallasHR and North Texas Relocation Professionals.

Volunteering is a great way to give back. I enjoy volunteering and being part of a team because it allows me to continue to meet new people, build current relationships, and achieve personal growth by learning from others. Including others on your journey provides resources and opportunities for you to share the experience.

Where are you volunteering your time? It might be time to take a new route to find an organization for you to give back and expand your network along the way. Ecclesiastes 4:12 says, "Though one may be overpowered, two can defend themselves. A cord of three strands is not quickly broken."

Developing a Network Requires Courage

I remember it like it was yesterday. When I was in my first year at Armstrong Relocation, my boss shared that I should get involved in some different organizations in my industry to expand my network. I attended several networking meetings and tried to find one that worked for me.

One of the first networking groups I decided to attend was a local SHRM chapter called DallasHR. I signed up for a luncheon meeting and prepared myself with some research on their website. I thought it might give me a chance to meet other HR professionals and learn more about their world since I worked closely with HR in my relocation role.

The day arrived and I drove about 20 minutes across the city to the hotel where the meeting was being held. I took a deep breath and walked into the event. I was overwhelmed when I saw over 200 people in the room talking with each other. It was loud, and the perception was that everyone seemed to know each other.

I didn't know anyone and had little success meeting other people that day due to my hesitation and uncomfortableness with interrupting or joining in on other conversations. I realized, however, the value of those conversations. I just needed to figure out how to meet some of those people and navigate through the organization.

Networking at events such as these can be a difficult process because you don't know anyone, and they don't know you. It's a lot like moving to a new town as a child and attending the first day of a new school. You haven't developed any friendships yet and the unfamiliarity with your surroundings is overwhelming. However, if you have the courage to get involved, it will make getting to know others a lot easier.

Networking Starts with Serving

When I first started networking, my approach lacked confidence. I would question myself about how I could possibly add value to others. I would often think "I am not an HR professional, or IT specialist, or whatever other professional is meeting together." Don't make that same mistake! This type of thinking will lead you to fear and doubt, as well as reduce your confidence around people.

The day you figure out ways to add value as a business professional will be the day networking will change your perspective and open doors for you that you would have never dreamed were possible.

Networking takes focus and a skill on serving others. When I was attending a local business networking event years ago, I remember at the end of the meeting when the facilitator asked everyone to stand up and exchange business cards for two minutes and try to see who could get the most cards. People would quickly shake your hand and literally throw their business card at you before moving on. It was like a tornado of business cards blowing in the room and you were just trying to get through it. This is NOT networking. Networking is about listening, learning, sharing, and being resourceful. It's also about serving others.

Perhaps you have experienced challenges when networking. Here are a few tips that might help change your route or direction when networking for maximum value:

Show up! When I decided to return for a second DallasHR meeting back in 2004, I pulled into the parking lot and remembered the overwhelming feeling I had experienced from the previous meeting. I felt anxious and nervous as I walked up to the hotel knowing that I was not going to know anyone in the room. Once I walked into the hotel doors, I looked over at the sea of people networking and immediately walked out of the hotel back to my car and started to leave. The anxiety kicked in. When I got back in my car, I took a deep breath and reminded myself that in order to meet people and connect with others, I had to muster the courage to show up and just be me. I am glad I went back into the meeting, because it impacted my business and personal relationships in a positive way for many years.

Be a learner. Focusing on the other person and being a good listener when networking is critical. We all know what it feels like when you have someone come up and introduce him/herself and just start talking about their business or their personal agenda. My wife and I attended a book signing years ago and met some great people. When we left, she mentioned that she had met a few really nice people and learned where they worked and about their family, but she also experienced an interesting observation. She said a person she was talking to never asked about where she worked. Many times we get caught up talking about our own situation and forget to focus on others. It reminds me of the quote by John Maxwell, "People don't care how much you know, until they know how much you care." Asking questions and being interested in others will deepen the connection every time.

Add value. A lot of people struggle with this area because they aren't prepared or don't feel like they have anything important to share. Adding value starts with learning and then sharing to be a resource to others. One way to add value is by connecting people you meet with people in your network. When I am networking with someone I have just met and then see another person I know, I try to introduce them so they can connect. People appreciate and value a good personal connection. I also try to learn as much as I can from that person so that I grow and share with others for their growth in their business and/or their personal life.

Networking is about a commitment to serving and takes work. It's a skill that everyone should work on to develop. The payoff is PRICELESS.

Is it time for you to change lanes and start networking with others? Write down some questions you can ask at your next networking event. Focus on what others may be looking for or a problem you might be able to help them resolve and then follow up with a solution. You will be amazed at the results!

Be In the Moment

One of the things I enjoy is networking with business leaders at local coffee shops. It's a great way to get away from the office and learn about people and some of the things they are doing for success. I always learn from others, but for maximum value, you must ask great questions and focus on the other person.

I have visited with people before who spend the whole time talking about their job, or business, or even dreams. This is great, but it felt like a waste of time since they didn't ask about me or ask how I might be able to help them. So remember, it's a two-way street!

Knowing a little about the person you're meeting with beforehand can be very helpful. A simple search on the Internet can often provide you with some useful information. Preparing a list of questions ahead of time can also guide you through the conversation and help you gain the most value from the meeting. Some of these questions might be:

> Tell me about your journey?
>
> How do you add value to others in your company?
>
> What are you currently reading?
>
> Who do you know that I should know?
>
> How can I add value to you or someone you know?

It's also important to prepare answers to questions such as these in case someone asks them of you. Most importantly, follow up when the meeting is over and make sure you do what you say you will do. This is where the MAGIC happens.

When the people you meet with see that you are focused in serving them, they will look at you with more credibility and be more open to serving you.

Add VIPs to Your Network

I was having dinner with my wife one evening listening to her share a story that she heard at a teacher's conference. The person speaking was talking about how using VIP principles can IMPACT you as a leader. I immediately thought about how this can be applied to all areas of business as well as one's personal life.

The following are the leadership principles behind the acronym VIP:

> Be **VISIBLE**. As a business leader, it's important to BE VISIBLE within your company. It's critical for each of us to walk around our workplace and connect with other team

members during the day to understand challenges employees are facing, to ask questions, and to be seen as a leader that cares about helping people.

Be **IN** the moment. We all get busy with meetings, projects, and day-to-day activities. While each of us is busy dealing with various issues, it's so important to focus on being IN the moment for impact. Pausing to ask questions to clarify and understand is key before moving to the next task.

Be **PREDICTABLE**. When I describe people as being predictable, I often use the word consistent. We all know when people are consistent, right? They are on time, they show up with a good attitude, and are consistent when making a commitment. People appreciate leaders that are PREDICTABLE in their approach when working with customers, business partners, and employees.

Focusing on the VIP principles can help elevate your leadership in both your professional and personal life. Be intentional with your VIP approach today when connecting with others and you will experience growth in your leadership, AND be a great example for others looking to grow.

Chapter 5 Summary

Let's pull over and review…

The Carpool Lane

Do you have a strong network today, or do you wish you had others to lean on for support? Remember that people like to help others, but they just need to know how. This may be a time to change routes and strengthen your personal network. Some of the questions to consider before moving to the next chapter include:

1. Who is in your network today?

2. Which of those people can you send a written letter to?

3. What value can you add to others when networking? What are some questions you can ask?

Fuel for Your Journey

Don't wait until it's too late to pick up some passengers to elevate your experience along your journey. Now is a great time to check out local networking groups in your area or industry to expand your personal network. Take action today to find one and then attend it! Follow up by writing down a list of three to five people that impacted your experience and schedule time in your calendar to write and mail them a personal note. They will be so thrilled, and so will you. Always remember that networking starts with serving. Add value to others first! Show up and be a learner and be in the moment. The journey is so much better when you find others to ride along with you.

> *"One of the best reasons for keeping quiet is it can't be repeated to anyone."*
>
> **–Lillian V. Fults**

DRIVE WITH PURPOSE

"Not everything that counts can be counted,
and not everything that can be counted counts."

–Albert Einstein

When you drive or lead with purpose, you are committed. Commitment is the key to getting through the tough days and making it to your destination. You can't be half in or even 90%, you have to own it!

Whether it's finishing college, advancing in your career, or improving your marriage, you will need to be committed all the way for the most effective results.

Playing to Win Puts You in a Different Lane

In 2003 I decided to take a position with Albert Moving in Wichita Falls, Texas, as the general manager. The company had been established for many years and I was hired to come in to hire, train, and motivate a team to help grow the company.

When I arrived, things were going great. I was able to bring some ideas and different perspectives from my past experiences, and everyone seemed happy. But by the time I got to month three, I wasn't enjoying my role as much and became disengaged. I just accepted the status quo and each day as it came.

After about six months, my boss asked me to visit with him and shared some of his observations and disappointments with me and some things he felt I should focus on to improve my performance in the area I was leading. However, there was one thing he said that stood out that helped me to change. He said, "It's like you are playing not to lose and not playing to win."

Though I felt frustrated after that meeting, it helped me to realize how uncommitted I was to the new company. The role I was responsible for just wasn't my lane. I was commuting 100 miles each week to work and my home still hadn't sold. This created motivation for me to look for a new opportunity back in Dallas and try something new.

In this case, change was painful but opened a new door for me that helped me find my lane in my career. Have you ever been in a situation where you didn't feel passionate, or enjoy being there? It is often difficult to make a change, but when you do, you have the chance to find a lane that allows you to use your talents and experience more joy in your life.

Burn the Boats

There is a story about a Spanish army that sailed to an island to take on a mighty army of warriors. The leader told the men to burn the boats so they would be committed to fighting for their life. There was no point of return—either fight for what you want, or die! Now that's pretty brutal. However, it is necessary to be totally committed in order to achieve your goals and dreams.

When I moved to Dallas, I burned the boats. There was no point of return because we were committed to making Dallas our home to give us the best chance at success for our family. It's the same concept in your job. If you take a job but aren't committed to making it work, it probably won't last long.

What about volunteering for an organization, or getting a new certification? When you play to win, you are leading your life with purpose. It blocks the thought in your head about quitting, or retreating when life gets difficult.

There were many times in the early years of my career that I would think about retreating and moving back, but then realized I had made a commitment and the boats had been burned, so I needed to change my thought process and grind through the difficulties in life to make it work.

Are you having challenges in your career? Are you committed to driving through the difficulties, or do you have the mindset of whatever works out? It may be time to burn the boat and commit to driving through the challenges until you achieve the desired results. If not, find the lane that gets you where you want to go, then BURN THE BOAT!

Playing to Win Requires Asking for Feedback

When you decide to make a commitment to something important to you, it often includes asking for and receiving feedback from people you know and trust to make decisions. Sometimes the feedback isn't really what you wanted to hear. Remember those report cards in school with the comments for improvement? Or the grade you received in college that was less than what you felt you earned? It's the same thing in your job. Feedback can provide you with a different perspective and direction to help you change lanes or just accelerate.

I'm not saying that when you receive negative feedback that you should leave your company. What I am saying is that when you receive negative feedback, you just need to shake it off and take whatever lesson you can from it so that you can get back in the game to improve your skills and find a different route.

I once had a conversation with my friend, Shelley Zajic, who said, "Feedback is a gift." Whether it is positive or negative, you should be open to listening and use the information to continue your growth. Sometimes this feedback will open your mind to new ideas and possibly help you find the lane that works best for you.

Playing to Win Requires Faith

In 2006, the Oklahoma Sooners earned a trip to the Big 12 Championship game to play the Nebraska Cornhuskers in Kansas City, Missouri. However, the Sooners did not know they would be playing until the week before when the Texas Longhorns lost to Texas A&M in the last game of the regular season. During that weekend, my oldest son surprised me with an early Christmas gift—two tickets to the Big 12 Championship Game in Kansas City.

I remember thinking how this was one of the greatest gifts that I had ever received. It was an opportunity to experience a trip to a college football championship game with my oldest son. I had a lot of emotions that week. I was definitely surprised and excited about the event, but also unsure and concerned about the trip knowing it would be snowing. Driving from Dallas to Kansas City would normally take 7 to 8 hours, but it would be much longer in snowy weather. I was also concerned about getting a hotel at the last minute.

As I thought about everything through my own lens, I began thinking about how much easier it would be to stay home and watch the game in the comfort of my living room next to a warm fire. Fortunately, I did not succumb to those thoughts.

With the help of my good buddy, Steve Dillie, who worked for Southwest Airlines, I found myself in Kansas City the following week. He made it possible for me and my son to fly standby instead of driving. We then met Patti Farr, our rental car representative, who not only assisted us with our car rental, but also exceeded our expectations by helping us find a closer hotel by the stadium.

The Sooners went on to defeat the Huskers in one of the coldest football games I have ever attended. But it was a special moment I got to share with my son and one I will always remember.

I share this personal story because it aligns many times with our professional and personal lives when we want to stay in our comfort zone and fail to find the courage to take a leap of faith.

My favorite word for 2016 was *vulnerability*. Being open to the perspectives of others requires a certain level of vulnerability. Let this year be the year you open yourself to being more vulnerable and listen to other people's points of view. After hearing these different perspectives, make the commitment to apply what you learned and drive with purpose on your journey for success.

Looking Ahead

We talked earlier about the importance of feedback. One of the things that I do every year is reach out to some of the most successful people I know and ask them if they have any plans for personal growth. Some of the questions I ask are centered around the following:

> What are some of your daily disciplines that help you focus each day?

> What are you reading that I should read?

> What do you do for personal development and continued growth?

> Is there anyone in your network that I should also connect with?

> What questions are you asking to make connecting more purposeful?

One thing I've learned over the years is that people love to share. It's a way for them to feel like they are adding value to others. To gain from this shared value, write down some questions and drive your next meeting with purpose.

Play to Win with People!

One of my favorite shows to watch on TV is a series called *A Football Life*, which portrays different people who have coached or played football. It's interesting to watch stories about the challenges these leaders and players faced, and how each person struggled through their challenges and overcame adversities.

Each player and coach on the show has experienced different kinds of adversity from family situations to being surrounded by the wrong people and even getting fired from their jobs. However, they all seem to have a purpose that allowed them to continue driving for success. There are a couple of common threads I see with each story that can be applied to all of us.

The first is to **work** hard. I once heard someone say the more you practice, the luckier you get. The best are never satisfied with being good, but always looking for ways to be better. What can you do to elevate your area of responsibility? Be unselfish. The most successful people focus on helping others improve and give credit to the team when achieving success.

The second is to **care for others.** Great leaders know their team members and their families and how to inspire them. What are you doing to show how much you care for others? Ask the question, "How I can add value to help you?" When people know you care, they will do more for you. Don't be embarrassed to say I love you and I appreciate you.

Great leaders are not afraid to say, "I'm not perfect," or to acknowledge needing each teammate to win as a team. Do you tell others how much you love and appreciate them? If not, consider taking a different route and deepen your relationships with a purpose.

Don't Compare Yourself with Others

When I started working at Armstrong, we had one of the top sales professionals in the nation working in our office who was a master at entertaining clients. It was one of the reasons for his success.

I once attended a national conference with him when I was in my second year and watched how he connected with so many others. He would take clients out and entertain them through the late hours in the evening. He drove a new vehicle, had a golf membership at a country club, and lived in a nice home.

After evaluating his approach, I thought I might need to start doing things differently to achieve success in my position within the company. But after careful consideration, I realized this just wasn't my lane. I had taken this position to have more autonomy, make a reasonable living for my family, and have a purpose in my life. It wasn't to become the top sales guy and make the most money. My goal was to add value to others around me. I needed to find the lane that worked best for me.

I once heard that "comparison is the thief of joy." When you compare yourself to others, sometimes it can make you feel better—especially when you compare yourself to someone who hasn't found their lane yet—and sometimes it can make you feel worse.

My brother in law, Earl Reynolds, is an excellent business leader. He has a great approach when it comes to measuring or comparing oneself to others—it's called the "mirror test." The way it works is you look in the mirror each day and ask yourself: Are you better today than you were yesterday? Are you growing, or shrinking? Are you engaged or disengaged?

Some of the best ways to avoid the comparison syndrome is to have an attitude of gratitude. Smile and look for the positive things in your life each day.

Chapter 6 Summary

Let's pull over and review...

Drive With Purpose

Are you all in? Being in your lane means you are 100% committed to your role to achieve results. If you aren't, it may be time to take a detour and figure out what you need to do to be committed so you are driving with purpose in everything you do. Some of the questions to consider before moving to the next chapter include:

1. Are you playing to win?

2. When is the last time you asked someone close to you for feedback?

3. When you look in the mirror, what do you see?

Fuel for Your Journey

When you drive with purpose, you are committed. Committed to your career, your relationships, and other important factors in your life. Driving with purpose also fosters patience and trust in the process. You will also be more open to giving and receiving feedback for improvement. This is how people grow in their career. Now is a great time to take the mirror test and have the courage to recognize when you need to step on the gas or take a different route to be all in!

> "A gambler's money has no home."
> –Dewey Ivey

CHANGING LANES

"The bigger the why, the easier the how!"

–Jim Rohn

I have worked alongside some great people in my career. Many of them have enjoyed a great career in the same role in the same company for many years, while others have moved or promoted to different areas of the business. It's always exciting to see people grow and have success. However, there are times when people with great talent leave a company for a different role only to realize later that they left for the wrong reasons.

As an employee looking for change, leaving a company for more money can be a good thing, and sometimes not so good.

Time for a Change

In 2002, I was working 60 to 70 hours a week as the general manager trying to turn around a Dallas company that had been stagnant for many years. I had made some progress with operations improvement and was working on growing sales. After about 16 months of working really hard and long hours to make some headway, I went to my boss and asked him for a raise. He said no.

Unable to get the support I needed, I told my boss that I would be making a change if I couldn't get more money for myself and a couple of key people in my office. I knew I would eventually lose them, and if I did, I would have to start all over. My boss declined, so off I went to search for a new position.

Within a few weeks, I found a new opportunity in Wichita Falls with a great offer. When I shared with my boss that I was leaving and was able to get a 50% increase in pay, he said something that eventually became a defining moment for me in my life. He said, "It will never be about the money." My response: "It sure does help though."

I really didn't understand the leadership lesson at the time, because I was thinking that I needed a raise and wanted more money to pay my bills and support my family. The lesson I learned was that it really wasn't about the money—I was just in the wrong lane.

I was trying to manage a $3 million company and didn't have the experience or support I needed to make the most impact. In other words, I felt like I was trying to paddle upstream without a paddle.

Jim Rohn once said, "The bigger the 'why' the easier the 'how'." I didn't have a big enough 'why' to keep it going so I decided to change my route. However, that would change a few years later when I learned the reason for leaving was really MORE than the money.

Many times we get bored or lose interest in our jobs and decide to make a change. People typically make a change at a time of inspiration, or desperation. Whatever it is that you decide to do, the biggest thing you need to know is your WHY. When you know your why, you will believe in yourself and feel confident in your journey.

Little Things Lead to Big Things

Have you ever looked at an opportunity knowing that it could be big someday? Many entrepreneurs will take risks and invest all of their resources in companies because they have a belief that it will grow into a big company for a big payoff in the future.

When I took the job at Armstrong in 2004, I was reminded of this principle. I was going into this position making much less money than I had made in the previous five years. However, this time was different. I was motivated to succeed in a different role and realized why when I helped my first customer.

I had received a call from Neil Plunkett, a good friend that told me his banker needed to move his mom out of a nursing home in Dallas to Houston. I went to meet the customer and was able to help him with the move. This was a very small move and didn't pay me that much, but I didn't care, because I was able to help someone with their need and bring in revenue for our company. It was exciting! I believed that I could do it and, most importantly, wanted to do it to prove to myself that I could succeed. It was more about the WHY.

This new sales position would give me autonomy and the ability to adjust my schedule around my kids' events so that I could attend football games, baseball practice, tennis matches, etc. This position would also give me access to a different network and business leaders to learn from.

This is when I knew that I had found my lane. I wasn't worried about the money because I knew that if I had some success, the money would follow. I even posted a quote on my wall in my office from Ray Kroc, founder of McDonalds, who said, "If you work just for money, you'll never make it, but if you love what you're doing and you always put the customer first, success will be yours." This quote reminded me to keep focused on serving the customer and the money would take care of itself.

There may be a time when you feel like you should make more money, and that may be accurate. However, the timing may not be right, or you just haven't shown the leadership team enough value to warrant a raise, or you may just not be in your lane and it's time for a change. When evaluating these types of decisions, it's important to get feedback from the people closest to you. This can help you better decide if you need to change your route or keep moving forward.

Making Things Happen

My wife is a "make it happen" type of person. She enjoys finding old furniture for a deal, then restoring it with a little sandpaper and paint. When she sets her mind on something, it happens. It is how she's wired.

My wife recently purchased some barstools that she wanted for her kitchen. She picked them up late at night and they were finished the next day. Why is this? I know she has a lot of other things on her to-do list. It's because the WHY was huge and the HOW was small. It was something she really wanted to get finished. Things get easier when you know why you want to do them.

The same thing happened when I decided to work at Armstrong. Sales may seem hard for some people, but for me, it was more than sales. It was a calling to help others. It was about having autonomy to create time to do the things I wanted to do in my personal life with the opportunity to help people along the way as a business advisor.

There's a quote by Mary Kay Ash that I often tell my children: "There are three types of people in this world: those who make things happen, those who watch things happen, and those who wonder what happened."

What are you doing to make things happen in your role?

Have a Work-Life Balance

How is your work-life balance? If you are like most people, it is good at times, and challenging at other times. We are all in a hurry; we are in a need-it-now kind of world. We often put pressure on ourselves to be all things to all people all the time.

When I was a young operations manager in Dallas, I was responsible for dispatching some of the moving crews early in the morning. So I would come into work early in the mornings to get a head start. One of the things about this position is that my inbox of paperwork would constantly pile up with invoices for approval and other expenses to code for accounting.

Early on, I would stay at work late just to get my inbox cleaned out. I enjoyed the feeling I got when I arrived in the morning to a fresh, empty inbox. However, I found myself not getting home until late and missing dinner with my family and running to my children's activities. So I decided to quit staying so late and come in a couple of hours early in the morning to get my inbox clear to begin the day. It worked better, but I found that no matter what I did, the inbox would be full once again by the end of the day.

When I spoke to some of the people closest to me with more experience, they gave me some great advice. They said the work will always be there, so focus on the things that matter most and everything else will take care of itself. This was easier said than done when trying to keep above water, but it helped me understand the importance of focusing on the most important things at work and in my personal life.

Our Chairman of the board, Tom Watson, shared some advice with one of our senior sales leaders that helped me put this into perspective. He said, "Ask yourself three times a day what matters to you in life, then build your life around that answer."

When you are faced with challenging issues or you are stressed because you can't get everything completed, try to focus only on the things that matter and everything will work out.

We are all striving for this balance in our life in some way. We try to balance our work schedule, kids' activities, volunteer activities, social events, and many other things including our health and fitness, our spiritual life, and our community life. But a person can only do so much.

I once heard Tony Hsuieh, CEO of Zappos, say, "It's not about work-life balance, but about work-life integration." This is so true!

Work life integration can be about sharing personal stories with coworkers at work, as well as sharing work challenges with friends away from work. Letting people know what you do, and who you are everywhere you go is a great way to align your professional and personal life.

I am not saying you need to start working at night after you clock out for the day. Absolutely not! You need to unplug for sure and focus on family and other things that matter to you. It's about being engaged the entire day with a focus on aligning your life's mission and purpose in everything you do.

Vision, Mission, and Legacy

Do you have a personal vision or mission statement? Is it written down? Several years ago I was planning some goals for the year when I started reflecting on the reasons the things I was trying to accomplish were important to me. I wanted to make sure each goal was in alignment with my life goals, my vision, and my mission in life.

During this process, I realized that I needed to make sure I understood WHY these things were important to me so I could understand and prioritize their importance for success. When you align your goals with your mission, the choices you have will be easier to make.

What's your vision? For example, I have a vision to be a business leader in the community. When I am planning my day, the activities that I focus on relate to my vision. This might include connecting with people, building relationships, reading the news, and listening to podcasts. To me, a business leader is someone people look to for resources when they have a challenge. So I make sure to look for ways to be resourceful when helping others. It's that easy!

What's your mission? My mission is to LEARN from mentors (books/people), GROW my talent, and SHARE resources to help lift others for maximum growth. For me, it boils down to learning, growing, and sharing. If I learn something new, I get excited as I know it will help me grow as a leader. Sharing what I know with others inspires me because I know it will help them too!

What's your legacy? One of the things I have struggled with is defining the legacy I want to leave behind. This is challenging for many people because we want to make a difference, but we are not sure what a legacy looks like unless you're a professional singer that makes hit records, or an athlete inducted into the Hall of Fame.

As John Maxwell discusses in his blog post, *What Should Be the Legacy of a Successful Leader?*, leaving an inheritance is when you leave something FOR someone, and leaving a legacy is when you leave something IN someone.

Life is short. Why not get intentional about WHY you want things in life, and who you want to be as you continue your journey. When your vision is clear, the choices are easy!

It's all about the why—know your why, and things will become clearer for you on your journey.

Chapter 7 Summary

Let's pull over and review…

Changing Lanes

Do you wonder why you are working at your job? When you finished college, it may be that you took a job to gain some experience, or simply because the job was close to home. Knowing your why is what brings fulfillment in life. Right now may be a time to pull over and stop to make sure you understand why you are in your current situation before continuing on to your destination. Some of the questions to consider before moving to the next chapter include:

1. Have you been thinking about making a change in your life?

2. Do you have balance in your life? If not, what areas of your life are lacking your attention?

3. What is your vision in life? What is your mission in life?

Fuel for Your Journey

If you want to make a change, don't do anything before you know your WHY. One way to start is to write down your reason(s) for wanting to achieve your next three goals. This will give you the motivation to push through the most important ones. Start small and work on being consistent. It's very difficult to be one way at work and one way at home. Finding the right lane is about being YOU everywhere you go. Have the courage to build your life around your vision, mission, and values. It makes your choices in life much easier. Write them down and use them as your compass each day to stay focused on what works best for you.

> "Don't be afraid to give up the good to go for the great."
>
> **–John D. Rockefeller**

MAKE THE MOST OF YOUR JOURNEY

"The best way to find yourself is to lose yourself in the service of others."

– Mahatma Gandhi

When we are serving, we are giving our time and resources to help others. We can serve in our workplace, in our community, and to our families at home. Serving people gives you an attitude of gratitude! Some of the best business leaders are those that have a servant's heart.

Invest in Others

Servant leadership is a philosophy and set of practices that enriches the lives of individuals, builds better organizations, and ultimately creates a more just and caring world. I have enjoyed the opportunity to work at Armstrong Relocation and Companies in Dallas, Texas under Mike Gonzales' leadership since 2004. I have always felt inspired to be around Mike as a business leader in the community. Mike is much respected in our organization because of his integrity and his ability to connect and serve others.

Have you ever had a boss that you enjoyed being around? What was it that made him/her special? I am confident that giving time, or giving advice, or just giving an ear to listen was one of the leadership traits along with integrity, caring, and being approachable.

When I first joined Armstrong, I knew right away that I had a chance to be successful because of the confidence Mike showed me in every setting. His words always centered around how could he help us get better, not only in our business, but in life.

Mike is one of the most positive and optimistic people I know. He is always sharing positive stories about how you can be a better person and ways to help others. His philosophy is to grow yourself, so you can share with others. Mike makes you feel like you can achieve success at the highest level when you invest in yourself.

There are so many leadership traits that describe Mike, but I would say the most impactful to me has been his generosity. Mike is a giver to many charities and people in need. Mike is pulled in many directions as a leader in our company and in the community, but he will always find time for his employees, especially employees on the front line in our organization.

I always say that we don't volunteer for positions to be recognized, but it is nice to recognize people that make a difference—and Mike has been a difference maker in my life and for so many others in the Armstrong organization. I like to say that I have a Board of Directors on my mentorship team, and Mike is one of them.

Who inspires you in your organization? Are they part of your Board of Directors to help you grow for success? Change your route and identify someone in your organization to let them know how you feel. Maybe even send them a book, or write them a personal note to let them know how their leadership has made a difference in your professional growth.

Make the Call

Have you ever wondered why some people have better relationships than others? Many times it is because we aren't taking action on what we could or should do. Let me illustrate…

When our family moved to Dallas in the 90s, we were about two to three hours away from our parents, which made it nice for a drive up when we wanted to connect. But with three active children in school, it often made it challenging to find time to visit, especially with a jam-packed sports schedule. However, I noticed my wife always made time to talk with her mom and dad on the phone, especially on Sundays. Like clockwork, her mom or dad would call on Sunday evening to catch up on the latest.

I didn't have the same routine with my mom and dad at the time and was kind of taken back by this consistency of connecting. I made a comment to her one day about this. She then said something that made impact. She said, "Well, maybe you need to make a call to receive one." BAM!

There I was thinking about why I wasn't getting something, when I should have been thinking about how I should be giving—it was time to make the call.

So many times we get stuck in a rut thinking about why things aren't happening for us instead of thinking how we can make things happen and take action for impact. After that conversation with my wife, I started being more intentional and reaching out to my mom and dad on the phone and have enjoyed some great conversations since then. When I changed my perspective and approach to giving, great things started happening.

Have you ever experienced a similar situation? Remember, it starts with you. Think about the people in your circle that you haven't heard from and what you can do to connect with them this week. It may be a much easier and more scenic route to take to get to your destination. It's your move!

The More You Give, the More You Get

"A devotion to serving others is one of the most important values in a man." I love this quote by George H.W. Bush. We all have strengths and the opportunity to contribute something to make this a better place for others. What is most interesting is that when you help others, you receive so much more.

Most of us have served others in some capacity by volunteering. I often get inspired when I hear about someone investing their often limited spare time to help support a charitable organization. I know some people that give a lot of money to their church, and others to their favorite charities that impact them in a special way.

There are often times people will be visible or tell you about the charity they are supporting, but most of the time you won't even hear about these people that make a significant impact in our society. Whether it is giving your time, or sparing a few coins for the local group raising money, GIVING makes impact.

I want to tell you about one person that inspires me for what he does for others. My oldest brother Mark has five children and many grandchildren that live in the Dallas, Texas area. He is the General Manager of his company and volunteers his time as a board member for a couple of different volunteer organizations in the community. Mark is also a devoted follower of Jesus Christ. He is active in his church and is a busy guy.

Many people in Mark's network know this about him and appreciate all that he does in his community. However, many people don't know that Mark also serves in a prison ministry on Monday night in Denton County, Texas. He has been doing this for a couple of years and is giving his time to drive his purpose to bring people closer to Christ.

When I say the more you give, the more you get, I mean when you give you should expect ZERO in return. However, most of the time it will impact YOU more than it impacts others.

Let me share a quick story to help drive this point home. Actually, I am going to let my brother Mark share this inspirational story with you for maximum impact:

> About three years ago, I began leading a Bible study in the Denton County Jail every Monday night for a couple of hours in Pod 18. A few months ago, I was asked to fill in at Pod 16 for someone who was going to be out for

two weeks. My first week in Pod 16, while leading the Bible study, I noticed a young man on the 2nd row who looked to be about 15 years old (he was actually about 21). He was older of course, he just looked really young. I noticed him because he had his chair tilted back on two legs and didn't really seem engaged. The next week I was back and the same kid was on the front row with all four legs of his chair on the floor. This week, he was engaged and even asked a couple of questions during the lesson. I returned to Pod 18 the following week and led a Bible study with the men with whom I had become familiar over the previous months.

When I notified the guard that I was ready to leave, my eyes met the eyes of the young man from Pod 16 (he had been transferred to Pod 18). When he saw me, he waved and started making his way toward me. I immediately began searching in my mind for his name. As he extended his hand for a handshake, his name came to me.

"Hi, Tommy, how are you?"

He answered by asking, "Are you in here every Monday night?"

"Yes I am."

"Well, great, I'll look forward to seeing you next week."

"I'll be there!"

So, I left the jail and went home. Upon my arrival at home, my wife Stephanie asked me how it went as she usually does. I told her I wasn't really sure, "Sometimes I wonder if I'm making any difference at all." She said she was sure that I was. Then I remembered that kid and told her, "There was a kid there who had been in Pod 16. I saw him as I was leaving and I even remembered his name. He seemed real excited to join the Bible study next week. So, something good did happen tonight."

On Tuesday morning I was sitting at my desk at work when I got a call from a friend. We're close enough that we know each other's spouses and pray for each other. I asked about his family and he ran down the list of how everyone was doing. I knew he had experienced a lot of problems with his son whom he had not mentioned. So I asked, "How's your son?" He said, "Well, he's still incarcerated. I'm not sure if I told you what is going on, but he is still in Denton County." Something clicked in my mind and I asked, "What is your son's name." He answered, "Tommy." I asked, "is your son about 5'10" with long brown hair?" And he said, "You know my son?" I told him I was a volunteer at Denton County Jail and his son Tommy had been in my Bible study the previous two weeks. He began to cry and repeatedly say, "Thank you for ministering to my son."

We had lunch together later that week and he shared that he had told his wife what had happened and she broke down in tears too. I learned that day that what I was doing was important. God can use me to make a difference in someone's life.

This is so inspiring and I am super proud of my brother and what he does for others. He invests his time to give and expects nothing in return. I know there are many others in this world that are also doing this and we wouldn't even know it.

When giving your time and/or money, it will get you in the right lane for maximum impact. The more it means to you, the more it will impact. Some of my most impactful moments in life have been when I served food during Thanksgiving for the Salvation Army, or when passing out hats to seniors at a senior community retirement center.

There is no better feeling than giving to others and making their world better with you being a part of it.

Be an Ambassador

In the DallasHR organization, there is a group of volunteers that help others get the most out of their experience when attending a meeting. This group is called the "Ambassadors." Their role is to help others connect with members and guests when sitting down for a luncheon. There are usually about 200 to 300 people at each event with about 8 to 10 people sitting at different tables.

Before the presentation begins, an ambassador will start the conversation by introducing themselves and sharing something about the organization. Then he or she will ask the next person to introduce themselves and where they work or something interesting about them.

This is a great way to help people get connected. You can also be an ambassador at work or in your community. When you meet someone and have an opportunity to share something that might add value for them, do it.

One of the most impactful times for me was when I was asked to be an ambassador at the HRSouthwest Conference in Fort Worth, Texas. This is one of the largest HR conferences in the country and always a great event for HR professionals to come together for educational sessions and networking.

We had started a Pair-n-Share program to help welcome first-time attendees to the conference. With approximately 2000 people in attendance, it can be overwhelming to someone new. The Pair-n-Share program helped by pairing someone with conference experience with a new attendee to help them navigate the conference for a great experience.

I think at the end of the day we all want to help people, and when you find your lane, you will enjoy being a great ambassador at your company, in a volunteer organization, or in the community. Being an ambassador is about being positive, resourceful, and willing to help elevate the experience for others around you.

Is it time to change your route? Try walking into your organization this week with a focus on serving others to help them get the most out of their experience. It's an amazing experience when you find your lane as an ambassador. As Darren Hardy says, "Be the Exception!"

The Goal is Bigger Than the Role

In high school, I always wanted to play quarterback. Our coach let me play quarterback for our offense that practiced to help make the first string defense better. I knew the ultimate role was to play the first string quarterback where I could throw that game-winning touchdown and lead our team to victory. But what our team needed was someone to run plays to help make our primary defense better. I just needed to realize that the goal was team first, and not so much the role I played.

It's the same way in business, or possibly in your community—there is a bigger outcome when the group pulls together and plays their role. Another word we often hear when talking about goals is collaboration. When the team pulls together, we are stronger and have a better chance of achieving big things.

What is your role and what can you do as a business leader or a leader in your community to help advance the group in achieving this goal? It may be assisting a salesperson with a new client, helping raise money for a charitable organization, or getting a community baseball field ready for the season opener. Whatever it is, know that the goal is more critical than the role.

10 Ideas to Make Impact

One day I was having coffee with a business partner and she mentioned that she was meeting with others to build her network. She was in transition and looking for her next leadership opportunity in HR. After our meeting she mentioned how much she appreciated the resourceful information I shared but didn't really know how she could add value to others.

What I told her was that everyone has something of value to offer. The key is to understand what the people in your network need to advance their profession. You can find this out by asking questions.

Adding value doesn't have to be difficult. Often times it's the simple things that make the greatest impact. The following are some of the things I do to make an impact on others:

1. Connect people to help them expand their network.
2. Share resources such as a quote or a story that made impact for you.
3. Write an article on something you are passionate about and share on social media.
4. Send someone you know a book that recently inspired you.
5. Smile!
6. Nominate someone deserving for an award.
7. Volunteer to help at a charity event.
8. If you know someone that is raising money for a charity, make a donation.
9. Call a friend to let them know you are thinking about them.
10. Send a personal note to someone that is on your mind.

I remember how it felt the day I received an unexpected package at work. It was a book with a personal note from Christie Linebarger, a friend I had recently visited with at her company. In her note she wrote, "Bruce, this book inspired me so much that I wanted you to have a copy too."

This had a significant impact on me. It was such a great feeling to receive such a small gift. It meant so much to me.

I have received several books from friends over the years that have helped shape my leadership. It is the power of giving! Everyone loves to give, they just need to know what others need.

Is your GPS leading you in the direction of being a giver? Think about ways to be a giver in your family, or community, or organization. Write them down and take action. It's a great lane to be in!

Chapter 8 Summary

Let's pull over and review...

Make the Most of Your Journey

Sometimes you have to stop thinking and start doing. What's your next move? There are many ways to serve and make impact as a giver in your workplace and in your home. Some of the questions to consider before moving to the next chapter include:

1. Do you focus on you, or do you focus on serving others?

2. Where are you serving?

3. Do you have a mentor?

Fuel for Your Journey

Think about something you can do to serve the people you connect with each day at work and in your personal life. To make the most of your journey, give much and expect nothing. When you see someone that might be struggling, refer a book, or send them an article that helped you. Always remember the goal is bigger than the role. Serve to make the team better, and keep learning along the way. Look for others over the next 30 days that you can learn from, someone that is willing to share and provide candid feedback to help you grow so you can change routes and find the lane that brings you joy.

Your time to lead is coming, so be prepared to change lanes.

> *"If you want to receive a call, then you might need to make one first."*
>
> **–Dana Maria Waller**

THE LANE OF FULFILLMENT

"If I have seen further, it is by standing on the shoulders of giants."

–Isaac Newton

We all need lifters in our life—those special people who provide support and encouragement during those times when we need it most. Equally important is ensuring that we lift others along the way. While that sometimes requires changing lanes, I have found this to be a lane of fulfillment.

The Value of a Lifter

One of my favorite scenes in the movie *Rudy* is when Rudy Ruettiger is upset and ready to quit the Notre Dame football team because he wasn't able to suit up for a game in his senior season. The scene shows Rudy standing in the stadium overlooking the field when his past supervisor and now friend comes over to talk with him about why he wasn't practicing with the team that day.

> Fortune: Hey, hey, hey, hey, hey what are you doing here, don't you have practice?
>
> Rudy: Not anymore, I quit.
>
> Fortune: Oh, well since when are you the quitting kind?
>
> Rudy: I don't know, I just don't see the point anymore.
>
> Fortune: So you didn't make the dress list, there are greater tragedies in the world.

Rudy: I wanted to run out of that tunnel for my dad to prove to everyone that I worked . . .

Fortune: PROVE WHAT?

Rudy: That I was somebody.

Fortune: Oh you are so full of crap. You're five foot nothin', a hundred and nothin' and hardly have a spec of athletic ability and you hung in with the best college football team in the land for two years, and you were also going to walk out of here with a degree from the University of Norte Dame. In this lifetime you don't have to prove nothing to nobody except yourself and after what you gone through if you haven't done that by now, it ain't gonna never happen, now go on back.

Rudy: I'm sorry I never got you to see your first game in here.

Fortune: Hell, I've seen too many games in this Stadium.

Rudy: I thought you said you never saw a game...

Fortune: I've never seen a game from the stands.

Rudy: You were a player?

Fortune: I rode the Bench for two years, thought I wasn't being played because of my color. I got filled up with a lot of attitude so I quit, still not a week goes by I don't regret it, and I guarantee a week won't go by in your life you won't regret walking out letting them get the best of you. Do you hear me clear enough?

I love this scene because it shows the value of friends who are also lifters in our life. They can help us see things from a different perspective.

Fortune was a lifter for Rudy. Do you have lifters on the route you are taking to your destination? Who have you encouraged lately to continue chasing a dream. Being a lifter is the ultimate lane to be in for success!

Everyone Has a Gift

Everyone has a gift to share with others. I have always been told that one of my gifts is encouraging others. I have been like this my whole life. I think one of the reasons it has been this way is because I enjoy how it makes me feel when someone lifts me up.

I can remember this starting as early as youth sports. My parents were big fans. My father coached me in youth baseball and my mom was always there smiling and encouraging me from the stands.

One year when I was playing little league football, I was playing defense and somehow recovered a fumble and got the ball back for our offense. Everyone was cheering as I ran off the field to allow the offense to take over. As I sat on the bench, my mom came over to tell me how proud she was and how she was going to buy me a 2-liter bottle of Dr. Pepper for recovering the football. I was in heaven! This was like the grand prize for a 7-year-old boy who knew he had just made an MVP play for the team.

I have shared this story with others as I have gotten older and still appreciate that moment. I don't remember the score—heck, I don't even remember what position I was playing or how much I even played. However, I do remember how it made me feel for my mom to smile and hug me and tell me I was getting a 2-liter bottle of Dr. Pepper.

A Simple Note

In 2009, I had been with Armstrong Relocation and Companies in Dallas for about five years and was starting to gain some tremendous traction as a sales leader. I was one of the top salespeople in the Dallas office and among the top 25% in the entire company of more than 100 sales professionals.

Our company has an exclusive group of sales leaders that are trying to qualify for the coveted Presidents Club each year—the top 10 sales leaders in the organization. Those who make the top 10 receive a trip to the annual convention at a nice resort with their spouse to celebrate their great year and to be recognized by the leadership team.

One day when I walked in my office, I found a copy of the previous year's convention brochure sitting on my desk with all the winners recognized. Along with the brochure was a note from our Vice President, Dave Nelson, which said: "Bruce, I thought you would enjoy seeing this program and look forward to seeing you as a Presidents Club honoree one day." This was impactful. It didn't say, we *hope* to see you here one day, it said they *looked forward to the day*.

When I received this, it helped me focus more than ever because Dave Nelson was saying 'I believe in you' and keep doing what you are doing and you will have success. Years later, I was able to share my gratitude with the leadership team when I was recognized in Colorado Springs as a first-time Presidents Club honoree. This was a special time that I will never forget.

So who have you lifted lately? Maybe it's time for you to reflect on people in your life that are working hard and trying to make a difference. That one lift can make all the difference for them. It will move you into a lane of fulfillment.

Maya Angelou, an American poet, says it best: "I've learned that people will forget what you said, people will forget what you did, but people will never forget how you made them feel."

It's About Opportunity

When I made the decision to join the sales team with Armstrong, I anchored my decision around something John Maxwell spoke to at a leadership conference I attended in Dallas, which was: When it's your dream, no one can talk you into it and no one can talk you out of it.

I started at Armstrong in 2004 with no business and 10 years later I was in Colorado Springs, Colorado with my wife for the annual Presidents Club awards dinner with about 50 people, from corporate presidents to national sales leaders. It was a special moment as I reflected on my journey over the last 30 years in business from working at my parents' bowling center to making a move to Dallas to be a staffing manger to taking a leap of faith and being recognized as one of the top sales leaders in the company. It was a moving experience, and I enjoyed reflecting on the journey when I accepted the award from Todd Watson, our CEO.

During the presentation each sales leader had the opportunity to share some words. When it was my turn, I spoke about success being all about the opportunity and expressed my gratitude to my colleagues and leaders in our company, and to my wife for her support and believing in me throughout my journey. I was overwhelmed with joy not because I had an excellent year, but because I had found my lane and was enjoying life to its fullest.

It's important to strive to be a better leader and person each day and appreciate all the people that pave the way for your success. Success is not about the money or the recognition; it's more about finding the best route for you to impact others. Everything else will follow!

I once received the following text message from my dear friend, Chrissy Conner, who is a great lifter:

How Big is Your Vision?

Is your God vision too small?

If your vision doesn't terrify you, then it is too small. A God vision should be so huge that you are bound to fail unless God steps in.

Is your God vision too narrow?

If your vision doesn't include others, then it is too narrow. A God vision has to include others like friends and teammates.

Is your God vision just a daydream?

If your vision doesn't get accomplished, then it is just a daydream. A God vision always gets done.

This message is a great reminder of the importance of dreaming big and stretching to make a difference in my life to help others. It's like a rubber band. When you don't stretch it, it has little purpose, but when you stretch it to tie up your hair or hold something together, it has significant purpose.

Are you dreaming big and stretching yourself to make impact? Right now might be a great time to change your GPS to find the route that leads you to something BIG.

'Be A Lifter' Leadership Interviews

In 2016, I committed to interviewing top business leaders to learn about their processes, grow from their wisdom, and share with others for education and growth. I have enjoyed reading, reflecting, and sharing some amazing leadership stories from some amazing leaders.

When I first started thinking about taking on this project, I shared my vision with others to get their feedback. Everyone thought it was a good idea, because it would serve different purposes from getting a successful leader in the spotlight to gaining and sharing insight on what makes this person such a great leader.

Many leaders believe that success is determined by the books you read and the people you meet. This is a testimony to my personal leadership growth over the past 20 years. I continue to learn each day by connecting with some of the most talented people in business.

The purpose of my leadership interviews is to add value by introducing people to leaders that make impact as they share challenges, successes, and perspectives on their journey as a business leader. Here are the 10 questions I asked the top business leaders I interviewed:

1. Where did you grow up?

2. How did you get started in your business/career?

3. Do you remember a challenge or life lesson that you had to overcome early in your career that made you a better leader?

4. What was that moment when you knew that you had found your lane, your purpose?

5. What is your favorite achievement in your current role?

6. Is there any one person that inspired or mentored you along the way?

7. Do you have a saying or mantra that you live by?

8. What book are you reading or listening to to help grow your leadership right now?

9. Can you share any of your daily disciplines that help you stay focused as a leader?

10. What advice would you give others to help them on their leadership journey?

I have received some great feedback and learned so much from these personal interviews. What's interesting and fulfilling is when these leaders tell me how much they enjoyed going through the exercise of reflection over their career. It's very clear that each person I interviewed also had lifters in their life that reminded them of the journey from their starting point to the leader they are today.

Each of these interviews can be found on my sales leadership blog "A Relocation Minute with Bruce Waller." If you'd like to see some of the responses I received during my interviews, visit my blog at **www.brucewaller.com**. They are impacting and can provide great guidance to finding your lane!

High Achievers Have Common Threads

I have been surrounded by some amazing people in my life, people who inspire me and who I call high achievers. When reviewing each leadership interview, I learned many didn't start in their lane and some leaders took longer than others to find what lane worked for them.

I have noticed that even though everyone has their own definition of success and achievement, there are many common threads among high achievers. Here are the top 10 lessons I learned from the top business leaders during my interviews.

1. Serve first.
2. Never stop learning.
3. Tell others they are appreciated.
4. Have a "nothing is ever accomplished alone" philosophy.
5. Mentors are key for growth.
6. Always evaluate where you are today.
7. Stay humble.
8. Have a "failing makes us better" attitude.
9. Add value to others.
10. Surround yourself with great people.

Do any of these lessons resonate with you? What's your favorite or most impacting? I encourage you to take some time and answer the leadership interview questions yourself, then reflect on your responses. Share your experience with others to help lift them and give them a different perspective. In doing so you just might help someone find a new route that leads them to their ultimate destination.

Mentors Give You Guidance

I have enjoyed sharing stories about some of the people that have helped me find my lane in my career. Many are still wonderful mentors in my life. Mentors can also be people that you have never met but wrote a book that made a difference in your growth.

I don't remember reading many books in high school, but over the last 20 years I have found reading to be a driving force in my leadership growth. I have learned so much from reading books and listening to audio tapes and podcasts in my car and while I am working out. In addition to inspiring you, reading can also instill ideas to act on and become a better leader.

Lifters remind me of a story about a young boy that was picking up starfishes that had washed up on the sand due to the low tide and throwing them back in the water to save them. A man observing the boy came up and mentioned how there were many starfishes that were along the miles of sand and it would be impossible to make a difference by picking these up and throwing them back in the water. The boy picked up the starfish and threw it in the water and looked at the man and said, "Well, it made a difference for that one."

This story demonstrates how one person can make a positive impact when he or she believes in making a difference. Does your current GPS take you along the route of lifting and impacting others? Part of finding your lane means staying focused on what you can do for others.

Find Your Lane to Say Thank You

Several years ago when watching the induction of the Football Hall of Fame, in Canton, Ohio, I thought about how great a stage these deserving men have to share their story and gratitude for the people that lifted them up from their time playing youth football to the professional ranks. These people often included family members, players, coaches, and long-time friends.

I know I will never make it to the pro Football Hall of Fame, but I decided to write an article and share it on social media about what I would say if I were given the opportunity to say thanks. The following is what I wrote:

Just in Case I Don't Make It to the Pro Football Hall of Fame...

I was recently inspired watching the Pro Football Hall inductees so much that I wanted to take the time to thank the people that have impacted my football life along this great journey! Thank you – Thank you – Thank you!

To My High School Coaches - Jack Tinsley, Jeff Pritchard, and Mike Snyder . . .

Football season was the greatest time growing up in Seminole, Oklahoma. Chieftain Pride! I was so blessed to have great coaches and players around me. It was a great experience! I was never the biggest, fastest, or strongest player, but I loved playing the game. It's been fun telling stories about how I tackled Troy Aikman in high school games, but I try not to mention that he struck me out more than once in baseball. Thanks to all of the coaches and players, as well as all of my classmates for sharing wonderful experiences . . . I recently reached out to thank my head coach for impacting my life with football. It was a great feeling to connect. If you haven't reached out to your HS football coaches lately, do it now! They would enjoy hearing from you and you will enjoy it too.

All of the Volunteer Coaches and Players I worked with from South Rock Creek to Lake Dallas . . .

All of the players and volunteer coaches that I had the opportunity to work with from South Rock Creek in Shawnee, Oklahoma to Lake Dallas, Texas . . . I hope you had a memorable experience in a positive way. Thank you for doing your very best at every practice and every game. I hope you learned half as much from me as I learned from each of you. Thanks for the opportunity to be there along for the ride. I will remember you guys forever and wish you all the very best.

Coach Michael Young, and the LD Quarterback Club

In 2005, I have had the privilege of being part of the Lake Dallas Quarterback Club. We all invested so much into this organization because we know how much a great program can impact a young person and their family. Thanks coaches for giving me an opportunity to be part of Lake Dallas Falcon Football family. Thanks for pushing our kids to be better and treating them with the utmost respect. I also want to thank ALL of the unselfish Quarterback Club volunteers I got to work with. You have truly made a difference in my life.

Michael Gonzales

I have enjoyed the privilege of working for Mike since 2004. Mike is not only a great leader for our company, but he understands the importance of family, and serving in our communities. Thank you for allowing me to have a job that I can have balance in my life which means never having to sacrifice my family and children events. Thank you for teaching me about leadership and for your encouragement to dream big!

Martha Ellen Causey Thornton

I am so thankful for my mom signing up my brothers and me to play youth football at a young age. I played for the Lions and Bears in Edmond, Ok in EASA… I don't remember any scores, but I do remember recovering a fumble one game and mom coming up to me to tell me how proud she was and she would be getting me a 2 Liter bottle of Dr. Pepper after the game! Thanks Mom for your continuous encouragement in life and for being my lifelong bowling partner!

Jack Howard Thornton

I was lucky to have my father always around for support when I played sports. He coached me in youth baseball for the Wildcats and always enjoyed talking sports. I always remember when I would be practicing as a freshman and varsity football in Seminole Oklahoma and looking across the practice field and there he was sitting in his yellow truck watching me while listening to sports radio and smoking his swisher sweet cigars... I know he was busy but he made time to watch practices and be at my games. Thank you for teaching me to be involved! I have since tried to carry on this legacy with my children.

Mark Waller, Joe Waller, Dean Thornton, Deborah Reynolds, Deanna Huff, Dawn Womack, and Mike Ivey

Mark and Joe, our year of coaching our kids together was one of the greatest years of my life. I am not sure how many games we won, but the experience was priceless. Thanks for a great experience. Joe, your involvement with videos for youth thru HS football and now the LD game day internet broadcast is so special. Thank you for your many sacrifices to bring the most exciting times to our program. We are going to miss this but will have great memories for the rest of our life! Mike, thanks for all of the conversations along the way. I really was inspired to watch your son play under you for Empire and Duncan. It was fun to watch and experience as family. Our family is so blessed to get together during the season to enjoy college football. It doesn't matter if we are for OU, OSU, North Texas, Texas Tech, or other college teams. It is something I have been able to pass on to my family. Thank you to all of my brothers and sisters for being great fans. You are the best brothers and sisters a brother could ever have. I love you all!

Adam, Allison, and Logan Waller

You are the best kids a dad could ever have. I am so proud of your character and values. I have enjoyed watching you learn and grow for many years. It's a great blessing and know you will understand the feeling when you have your own children. There is nothing better than watching your children succeed, and sometimes learning from failure. I hope you enjoyed playing sports as much as I did. Each of you have made great lifelong friendships, enjoyed competing, and enjoyed some fun trips with many of your friends along the way which still make for great stories. I love each of you and look forward to watching you teach your children if they decide to be involved in sports or other areas . . . .

Dana Maria Ivey Waller

To my beautiful wife, I was so blessed to marry a beautiful girl from college that is now my best friend. We have enjoyed a great journey. Sports is a big part of our life! From the youth sports to high school football --- Friday night lights is not just about football, it's about lifelong friendships we have made along the way. Thank you for your unconditional love. We have been truly blessed with three wonderful children and enjoyed watching our kids' football events for the last 20 years as parents, volunteers, and fans. Thank you for sharing the experience. I am thankful to you for volunteering me as flag football coach, and then later volunteering me for a Jr. High rep for the Quarterback Club... It has truly been a blessing knowing you were always right there with me. I Love you! I look forward to sharing more great memories during Logan's senior year with you soon!

In Conclusion—Remember, it's not how we start the race, it's how we finish. Get involved and strive to do your very best. Life is about character and contribution and you have a great opportunity to make a difference in someone's life! Thanks again for making a difference in my life.

Chapter 9 Summary

Let's pull over and review…

The Lane of Fulfillment

Are you a lifter or encourager to others when at home or at work? Being a lifter is about encouraging, listening, and serving others with your talents and resources. It might be something you say, or a message you share via text or email that gives someone you know the confidence to change routes on their journey. Some of the questions to consider before moving to the next chapter include:

1. Have you been around someone that lifted you up?

2. Have you taken the leadership interview?

3. What did you learn from other high achievers?

Fuel for Your Journey

Everyone has a story and needs a lift from time to time. Consider challenging yourself to encourage others when they are struggling. You could be the difference in their success. Take some time to invest in answering the "Be a Lifter" interview questions and reflect on your answers. It is an amazing exercise to go through as it will remind you of the many lifters in your life. Once completed, print it and put it in your journal, send it to a friend, or even send it to me. I would truly enjoy hearing about your experience. It might also be what you need to find your lane for success and fulfillment.

> *"We must find the time to stop and thank the people who make a difference in our lives."*
>
> **–John F. Kennedy**

Maintain Your Vehicle

"Perfection is not attainable, but if we chase perfection we can catch excellence."

–Vince Lombardi

A s we near the end of the book, I want to share the most important lesson to finding your lane. It starts with investing in yourself before you invest in anything else. Investing in yourself is a lot like keeping your vehicle maintained. You have to invest in the fuel, oil changes, tune ups and other routine maintenance to ensure your vehicle performs at its best.

Investing in Yourself is a Process

One of the ways I invest in myself is by exercising. I have enjoyed working out early in the mornings for the past ten years and have seen some great results. I remember when I first started how hard it was to get up out of bed to go work out. Someone once asked me what I liked most about working out, and I said, "When I am finished."

One thing I've noticed over the years is that the gym is always packed in January. In February the crowd thins out, and by June it's a ghost town. Why is this?

I believe the reason so many people fall short of their fitness and other goals is because they all want quick results. We all have a vision of what we want to look like, but we want it now. When we go to the gym, we want to see results after week one, but this is just not the case. It reminds me of a story I read in the *Compound Effect* by Darren Hardy. It's called the magic penny.

The story is about the choice to take a penny that doubles every day for 31 days, or the choice to take $3 million dollars cash on day one. Many people will take the $3 million cash because it is instant. However, if you know the story, the penny that doubles in value each day is the best choice. After day 5 you have 16 cents, after day 10 you have $5.24, and after day 20 you have $5,234. However, this is when compounding starts to make significant impact. When you get to day 29, the penny choice is at $2.7 million dollars, and on day 31 you've got over $10 million dollars!

How can we overcome our need for instant gratification? It starts with commitment—making the choice to stick with something for a set period of time.

Recently, I started a fitness boot camp that meets two times per week. It is super hard. There have been many times when I just wanted to skip the workout, but my goal and commitment to exercise for the next year helps me with the choices I make to get up and go.

The same can be applied to your job or your marriage. You've got to stay committed to the process and the larger goal at hand. It's a lot like the slogan from the old FRAM oil filter commercial—you can pay little now for an oil change and filter, or you can pay a lot later when you need to replace the engine.

When I started with Armstrong, I didn't have a 13-year-plan. I had a plan for each day, week, and month, with a target for the year. You take it day by day and try to get better at whatever you are doing.

In the book *Outliers*, Malcolm Gladwell talks about how we need to work on the same thing for 10,000 hours to become world class. He didn't say 10 hours, he said 5 to 10 years! It's important to know whatever you are trying to achieve, it starts with commitment and a belief in the process.

It's Easy Not to Do

There's a quote by Jim Rohn that says, "What is easy to do is also easy not to do." I believe this is one of the reasons so many people fall short of their goals—myself included. Allow me to share my own personal story.

In 2005, I decided it was time to start working out on a consistent basis. My brother Joe lived across town and had some workout equipment so we decided to start working out in the mornings to get more fit. I remember when we started, we were so energized and excited about the end results. We even named his garage Joe's Gym and posted it on social media. Some people thought my brother actually owned his own gym.

At each workout we would spend about 45 minutes together talking about fitness and life in general. I remember how easy it was to get up at first because it was something new. But once the newness wore off, there were many days when I found it very difficult to get out of bed and drive across town for a 45-minute workout. Eventually it became easier not to do the workouts, and I stopped going altogether.

When it comes to how you go about achieving the goals you set for yourself, you have to find what works for you. Driving across town to work out in my brother's garage did not work for me. But working out first thing in the morning does. I didn't learn this overnight, however. It took some trial and error to find my lane and achieve long-term success.

Make it Work for You

When it comes to investing in yourself, I believe exercise should be at the top of your list. Not only is it a great way to improve your physical and mental health, its life-altering effects can enhance all aspects of your professional and personal life. The key is to find what works for you.

Find Your Lane

When it comes to exercise, some people like to work out three to five days a week, while others do it five to seven days a week. Some people like getting up early to work out while others find working out at night works best. It doesn't matter if its morning or night, as long as you are committed to the process and taking the necessary action to achieve your goals. The key to success is doing what works best for you.

After I started exercising, my wife decided she wanted to start working out too. But she is not an early morning person so she decided to work out at night. So I decided to change my schedule to workout with her in the evening. But exercising at night just didn't work for me. It seemed like something would always get in the way. So I switched back to early mornings so that I could get my workouts done and out of the way. Since then, my wife has found her lane with a different program, and I do what works for me.

A lot of people say they can't work out early in the morning, and if you're one of those people, that's okay. Just find your lane, and commit to the time and days that work best for you. Maybe it's only one night per week and one day on the weekends when you first start. The key is to make a commitment and follow through to the end. Once you find your lane, it will quickly become a part of your weekly routine.

Another excuse people give themselves to not exercise is they don't have the time. Everyone has the same amount of time each day. It's what we choose to do with those 24 hours that makes the difference. I love the quote by Steve Gleason, who was known for blocking a punt on Monday Night Football on the night the New Orleans Saints returned to the Superdome after being evacuated in the midst of hurricane Katrina. He said, "Someday is today!"

Keep an Eye on Your Dashboard

If someone asked you which dashboard gauges on your vehicle were most important, you would probably say the speedometer and fuel

104

gauge. Can you imagine driving your car without knowing how fast you were going, or how much gas you had in the tank?

What about oil level and tire pressure? Thankfully our check engine light on the dashboard appears when there seems to be trouble ahead. These gauges are critical to helping us maintain the health of our vehicles so we can travel safely each day to our destination.

Though we don't have physical gauges to tell us when we need to refuel or fix something in our professional and personal lives, there are certain indicators or gauges we can look to on our hypothetical dashboards.

In relocation, we look to on-time pickup and deliveries by our van operators, survey accuracy for the moving estimate, and quality scores for best customer experience to just name a few. I know recruiters that focus on time to fill job requisitions, HR leaders that focus on engagement, and sales professionals that focus on the number of calls made each day.

Establishing a few gauges to focus on in your professional and personal life can help increase your chances of success. Such gauges can help you see when something isn't working for you and when it's time to make some changes. It doesn't matter if you're in an entry level role or part of the senior executive leadership team. To stay aligned with your professional and personal goals, you need to keep an eye on your personal dashboard.

Invest in Personal Growth

In 1997, I was challenged with an employee relations issue and really struggled with this situation as a young manager. I spoke with my brother about it as he had lots of experience with these types of issues. He handed me a cassette tape from John Maxwell's Maximum Impact Club called "Making the Tough Call."

I remember leaving the office and listening to this tape in my car all the way home. It was like riding home with a business coach in my car. I was immediately hooked on leadership development. The message from that cassette tape provided me with different perspectives and ideas when it came to dealing with people. After listening to the tape, I was able to solve the problem.

I had read leadership books before, but I didn't remember any of them being as impactful as the messages communicated in that casette tape. This led me to read *The 21 Irrefutable Laws of Leadership: Follow Them and People Will Follow You*, by John Maxwell. This book had a significant impact on my life; it is what started me on my personal growth journey at the age of 32. It was not only about how to lead in business, but included principles and strategies to lead yourself.

Since then, I have committed to a personal growth plan to grow in not only my career but also my personal life. I am so thankful for all of my mentors, which includes authors, speakers, and the people I learn from everyday.

Invest in Yourself to Inspire Others

One of my favorite books is *Coach Wooden's Leadership Game Plan for Success: 12 Lessons for Extraordinary Performance and Personal Excellence*, by John Wooden and Steve Jamison. There are so many great takeaways from this book, but one of the most impactful are John Wooden's seven principles. These are some of the values that were passed down to John Wooden by his father that he kept in his wallet growing up.

I have these seven principles on my wall in my home office, as well as in my wallet. I try to share them with others along my journey, sometimes including them in graduation cards as a personal note. They are a great life list to live by every day. The seven principles are as follows:

1. Be true to yourself.
2. Make each day your masterpiece.
3. Help others.

4. Drink deeply in good books.
5. Make friendship a fine art.
6. Build a shelter for a rainy day.
7. Pray for guidance and give thanks for your blessings every day.

Start a Journal

When my sweet grandmother Lillian Fults was dying of cancer back in 1998, my wife bought me a journal to write down my thoughts. She thought it might be a way to help me grieve and give me something to look back on. I have now been writing in this journal for over 20 years.

Do you have a journal that you write in on a consistent basis? Journaling can provide great insight into yourself and your life. Keeping track of your thoughts, ideas, and progress is also an excellent way to learn more about yourself. A journal can also be something you can share with your children or grandchildren one day so that they can get to know you better. It can even serve as a legacy and be given as a gift.

When you first start writing in a journal, it can sometimes be a struggle to know what to say. One of the ways to overcome this is to just write down what you did for the day or who you connected with. Always date the entry as well. This is something you will appreciate when looking back in time.

Writing in multiple journals can also be helpful. I have since started a leadership journal, sales journal, prayer journal, fitness journal, and now a book project journal. It's a great way to capture special moments from various aspects of your life to share with others.

A Journal for Someone You Love

Every time you invest in reading, you should always try to take at least one idea or strategy and apply it in your own life. This will elevate your leadership. We all learn so much more when we take notes and apply ideas that other people use in their process for success.

Many years ago I came across a story while reading *The Compound Effect*, by Darren Hardy, that gave me an idea that I thought would be great to give to my wife as a gift. Darren told a story where a friend was having challenges in his marriage and wasn't sure where to turn. Darren suggested he stop focusing on the problems and start focusing on all the good things his wife was doing for him. He advised his friend to journal each day at least one positive thing he saw in his wife. Some examples included the clean sheets she put on their bed each week, a cooked meal she prepared for their family, or a kind word or compliment she might have given him.

Darren's friend took his advice and began writing in a journal. After a year had passed, he gave the journal to his wife. He thought it would be a great gift for her, and it was, but he didn't realize the positive impact it had had on him and his marriage. It made him fall in love with his wife again.

I was moved so much by this story that I decided to journal the same things over the next 12 months for my wife. Each day I would use my notes in my iPhone to capture something she did or said that was positive. A couple of weeks before Thanksgiving, I went to the bookstore and purchased a nice leather journal and transferred all of my notes to the journal. It took me several lunch breaks during the week to complete. On the day before Thanksgiving, I invited my wife to dinner at Olive Garden (one of her favorite restaurants at the time) and gave her the journal as a gift. She loved it!

It is transforming when you focus on the positives in your life. It really lifted our marriage like never before. If you are in a rut, or want to create some elevation in your marriage, or with any part of your life, start with writing in a journal and focus on the positives. You will be amazed by the results!

The best thing that happened to me in college was when I met my beautiful wife Dana Maria Ivey. We were young and life didn't seem that easy as we were trying to find our lane as a young married couple. But over the years we managed to raise three wonderful children (Adam, Allison, and Logan) and have grown to love one another like never before.

Life can be complex and is full of choices that will lead you down different roads. My and my wife's road hasn't been easy, but we made it work and are happier than we have ever been because we made the commitment to make our marriage work no matter what challenges came our way. We had a slow start but have stayed focused on serving each other so that we can finish strong.

Investing in Yourself Leads to Excellence

It's always fascinating to watch world-class athletes from around the world compete for an Olympic medal and represent their country on the podium. Bob Bowman is the Olympic swim coach for Michael Phelps and for the US Olympic team. He recently wrote *The Golden Rules* to share leadership lessons for excellence from his journey with other athletes as a swimming coach. The story is about coaching and developing people to help them pursue their dreams to one day be in the Olympics. As we all know, Michael Phelps is now one of the most decorated athletes in Olympic history with 22 gold medals in his career, but it didn't happen overnight.

Being excellent is about having a process to improve yourself every day. Bob Bowman's process is called "The Method." He uses this process for training each athlete as they go on a journey to pursue their dreams of being a champion.

Being excellent also requires being committed or having an all-in approach to your dreams. It requires a game plan to align with your vision and being purposeful by doing the things that matter each day. Excellence also requires sustained effort to push you to improve something each day. Having a consistent development process will help you improve in all facets of life.

So ask yourself the question: What is my dream or something I really want to achieve? Invest some time to review and apply some goals to help you reach the next milestone. This action will create momentum for you as you pursue your destination both in your personal life and your career. Then ask yourself, "What's next?"

Chapter 10 Summary

Let's pull over and review…

Maintain Your Vehicle

When was the last time you took a class on personal growth in terms of your career, personal finances, or relationships? Today, finding ways to improve yourself is just a book or a YouTube video away. Find the courage to take a detour to find a better lane. Some of the questions to consider before moving to the next chapter include:

1. Which areas of your life do you want to experience personal growth?

2. What can you do to invest in yourself for personal growth?

3. What are some of the indicators/gauges you can use to monitor your progress?

Fuel for Your Journey

Maintaining your vehicle means investing in yourself in ways that promote personal growth and improved physical and mental health. It can be as simple as investing $5 to $10 on a journal and establishing a daily routine of writing down a few notes and thoughts. Incorporating exercise into your life is also important. Look at it as the fuel and oil your engine needs to keep you moving down the road. The key to achieving personal growth is to be committed to the process. Steer clear of the pitfalls of immediate gratification and merge into the lane of lifelong results.

> *"Your success in the next 5 years will be determined by the books you read and the people you meet."*
>
> **–Jim Rohn**

CONCLUSION

FIND **YOUR** LANE

"A bad attitude is like a flat tire, you can't go anywhere until you change it!"

–Anonymous

When it comes to finding your lane, remember—it's not how you start, but how you finish. What do you need to finish? Perhaps it's time to finish your education or get that certification you have been thinking about. Or maybe it's about just taking action to pursue that dream job, or putting a plan together to achieve your financial goals.

Each leadership lane can only be recognized by facing and taking action. We all have challenges along our journey, but when you begin building meaningful relationships, and surrounding yourself with great people, the adversity will be easier to overcome. It will get tough at times and things won't always work out the way you want. But you'll just have to shake it off. Many of the challenges you'll face will serve as reasons to do better. If you make some wrong turns along the way, learn from your mistakes and get back on course.

Let me conclude with a personal story about how sometimes you just need to pick up the pieces and move on.

One of our family traditions is playing golf each year with our family on the 4th of July. I have been playing with my uncles for over 25 years and always look forward to spending time with each of them. My uncle Walter recently passed away to join his mother and father in heaven and it reminded me of a leadership lesson he taught me on the golf course.

It was several years ago when my son (Logan), my brother (Joe), and his son (Tyler) were playing golf with our uncles, Floyd, Dave, and Walter and several cousins. We were all divided into different groups. My uncles were in one group and my brother and I and our sons were in the group behind them. We were all having a great day chasing the little white ball over the course. At the time, our sons were only novice golfers learning to play, but they enjoyed playing golf. We even let them drive the cart, which they liked even more.

We were finishing our last few holes when my son was driving up to the 17th hole where my uncle's golf cart was parked as they were teeing off on the hole in front of us. We had just finished hold 16 and when we were pulling up to park behind my uncle's cart, my son's foot slipped off the brake and hit the gas, and we crashed right into the back of my uncle's golf cart. Thankfully no one was hurt, but the plastic wheels on my Uncle Walter's pull cart (this is a golf bag holder with wheels so you don't have to carry your golf bag while playing) were completely shattered. I felt so bad for my son since it was an accident, and felt terrible for my Uncle Walter's golf cart. I can see him now as he got out of the cart and started picking up each little shattered piece as he said, "It's okay, Logan, I think I can glue it back together."

This is how my Uncle Walter was, kind and compassionate even when he knew there was absolutely no way to put those shattered pieces back together. When I mentioned to Logan that he couldn't put the pieces back together, but we could do the right thing and re-place the damaged cart with a new one, that's exactly what we did right after we finished our round of golf.

The best route to take on your journey always starts with taking ownership. You will make mistakes along the way, but it's how you respond to those mistakes that makes the difference. Sometimes things get damaged, including relationships. Being mindful of others and trying to look at things from the other person's point of view will help you recover easier when these things happen.

Sometimes finding your lane means starting over in your career or in your relationships. As John Maxwell says in his book, *The 21 Irrefutable Laws of Leadership*, sometimes you have to "give up to go up"—that's the law of sacrifice. In other words, don't be afraid to take a step back to move two steps forward.

Some people find their lane early in life, while others might go through several jobs to find their lane. However, each job provides a life experience and leadership moment to learn from, but most importantly helps you build relationships with others. I always go back to Proverbs 27:17 when I think about the importance of being surrounded by great people. It says "As iron sharpens iron, so one person sharpens another."

I have enjoyed watching my children grow up in a small community in Dallas, Texas and develop great friendships on their journey. My oldest son Adam has found his lane as a sales leader in Dallas. He is married to his wonderful wife Alexia, who has found her lane in the medical field as a pathologist. My daughter Allison found her lane early on as she pursued the nutritional science field at Texas Tech University, and later completed her Master's degree at Oklahoma State University. She is currently a Registered Dietician in Dallas, serving people looking to improve their health and wellness. She is married to a great guy, Chase, who found his lane in the construction industry building large projects in Dallas. My son, Logan, recently graduated with a finance degree from University of North Texas and found his lane in the finance industry.

I found my lane when I met my wife Dana in college. She has shaped not only my leadership, but my direction in life and helped me focus on things that matter most. Dana serves as the Childcare Program Director for the Lake Dallas Independent School District. I remember when my youngest son was 1 to 2 years old and my wife would say, "He is not going to be young long. Enjoy the moments because they go by fast." Then I blinked and each of my kids are now all adults.

Indeed, time goes by fast—don't blink! Since I started writing this book, my daughter gave birth to a baby boy, our first grandson named Crosby. I know he will grow up fast too.

My hope is some of these leadership principles have inspired you or given you at least an idea to put into action to help you find the best route to help elevate your success in business and your personal life. As I close, I want to leave you with a quote I received from Jimmy Taylor, a business consultant who served with me on the DallasHR Board of Trustees. The poem is by Wilferd Peterson, author of *The Art of Living*:

> *"Walk with the dreamers, the believers, the courageous, the cheerful, the planners, the doers, the successful people with their heads in the clouds and their feet on the ground. Let their spirit ignite a fire within you to leave this world better than when you found it...."*

Find YOUR lane and be a lifter for others!

ABOUT THE AUTHOR

Bruce W. Waller is the Vice President of Corporate Relocation for Armstrong Relocation and Companies in Dallas, Texas. Bruce graduated from the University of Central Oklahoma with a degree in Business Administration. He has enjoyed many roles in relocation from operations to general management since 1995. Bruce is certified by WorldwideERC as a Certified Relocation Professional (CRP) and serves on the North Texas Relocation Professionals Board of Directors.

In 2014, Bruce was the recipient of the Saul Gresky Award presented to NTRP's Relocation Professional of the Year. Bruce is also certified by the HR Certification Institute (PHR) and the Society of Human Resource Management (SHRM-CP), and he currently serves as the Chairman for DallasHR Board of Trustees, one of the largest local SHRM chapters in the country.

Bruce has three children and lives with his wife Dana in Little Elm, Texas.

To learn more about Bruce, visit **www.BruceWaller.com**.

SOu

Introduction

1. Keepinspiring.me. *100 Most Inspirational Sports Quotes of All Time*. Retrieved from http://www.keepinspiring.me/100-most-inspirational-sports-quotes-of-all-time/#ixzz4kvg55eq8

Chapter 1

1. BrainyQuote. *Mark Twain Quotes*. Retrieved from https://www.brainyquote.com/quotes/quotes/m/marktwain118964.html

2. Sandler, Doug. Twitter post: "If it is to be it is up to me." Retrieved from https://twitter.com/djdoug?lang=en

3. Wikipedia. *Blake Treinen*. Retrieved from https://en.wikipedia.org/wiki/Blake_Treinen

4. *The Rookie*. John Lee. Walt Disney Productions., 2002. Film.

5. TED. *Matt Cutts: Try something new for 30 days*. Retrieved from https://www.ted.com/talks/matt_cutts_try_something_new_for_30_days

6. Anonymous. *The Man in the Glass*.

7. MercyMe. "Dear Younger Me," from *Welcome to the* New. Song. Fair Trade/Columbia, 2014. Lyrics retrieved from https://www.google.com/search?q=dear+younger+me+lyrics&oq=dear+yo

119

Chapter

1. Goodreads. *Quotable Quote: John Wooden.* Retrieved from http://www.goodreads.com/quotes/203719-the-true-test-of-a-man-s-character-is-what-he

2. Carnegie, Dale. *How To Win Friends and Influence People.* New York: Simon & Schuster, 2009.

3. Rath, Tom. *Strengths Finder 2.0.* New York :Gallup Press, 2007.

4. Watson, Jim. Quote: "Every day is a good day and some days are even better."

5. Maxwell, John C. *Today Matters : 12 Daily Practices to Guarantee Tomorrow's Success.* Warner Faith, 2004.

Chapter 3

1. QuoteAddicts. *"Your actions are so loud I can't hear you."* Ralph *Waldo Emerson.* Retrieved from http://quoteaddicts.com/i/5193413

2. Ortberg, John. *If you want to walk on Water, You've Got to Get Out of the Boat.* John Ortberg, 2001.

3. Singletary, Mike. Allied Van Lines Sales Conference, 1999.

4. Byers, Phil. Miami Herald article. Date Unknown.

Chapter 4

1. Great Inspirational Quotes. *Motivational Zig Ziglar Quotes.* Retrieved from https://www.pinterest.com/pin/189573465534957318/

2. Success Magazine. *Interview: Kevin O'Leary.* Success Magazine CD. Success.com.

3. Hardy, Darren. *Darren Daily*. Video. Retrieved from https://www.darrendaily.com

4. Robin Roberts say that her mom would always tell her to "make her mess her message." Speech during ESPY Awards July 2013 'Make your mess your message,' "

5. *When the Game Stands Tall*. Thomas Carter. David Zelon, 2014.

6. Holtz, Lou. *Winning Every Day: The Game Plan for Success*. New York: Harper Business, 1998.

Chapter 5

1. BrainyQuote. *Top 10 Franklin D. Roosevelt Quotes*. Retrieved from https://www.brainyquote.com/lists/authors/top_10_franklin _d_roosevelt_quotes

2. Success. *Tom Izzo on Inspiring Your Team*. Retrieved from http://www.success.com/podcast/tom-izzo-on-inspiring-your-team

3. Business Insider. *You're The Average Of The Five People You Spend The Most Time With*. Retrieved from http://www.business-insider.com/jim-rohn-youre-the-average-of-the-five-people-you-spend-the-most-time-with-2012-7

4. BibleHub. *Ecclesiastes 4:12*. Retrieved from http://biblehub .com/ecclesiastes/4-12.htm

5. Goodreads. *Quotable Quote: John C. Maxwell*. Retrieved from http://www.goodreads.com/quotes/1358055-people-don-t-care-how-much-you-know-until-they-know

Chapter 6

1. The Quotation Page. *Quotation Details: Quotation #26950*. Retrieved from http://www.quotationspage.com/quote/26950.html

2. Success. Quote by Sara Blakely. Success CD. Success.com.

ll Life. TV series. NFL Productions, 2011.

1. Goodreads. *Quotable Quote: Jim Rohn.* Retrieved from http://www.goodreads.com/quotes/855377-the-bigger-the-why-the-easier-the-how

2. BrainyQuote. *Ray Kroc Quotes.* Retrieved from https://www.brainyquote.com/quotes/quotes/r/raykroc173414.html

3. Goodreads. *Quotable Quote: Mary Kay Ash.* Retrieved from http://www.goodreads.com/quotes/600774-there-are-three-types-of-people-in-this-world-those

4. Success. Tony Hsuiech interview on Success CD. Success.com

5. Maxwell, John C. *What Should Be the Legacy of a Successful Leader?* Retrieved from http://www.johnmaxwell.com/blog/what-should-be-the-legacy-of-a-successful-leader

6. BrainyQuote. *John D. Rockefeller Quotes.* Retrieved from https://www.brainyquote.com/quotes/quotes/j/johndrock119902.html

Chapter 8

1. Goodreads. *Quotable Quote: Mahatma Gandhi.* Retrieved from http://www.goodreads.com/quotes/11416-the-best-way-to-find-yourself-is-to-lose-yourself

2. Bush, George W. *41: A Portrait of My Father.* United States: Crown Publishing Group, 2014.

3. Vimeo. *Darren Hardy: Be the Exception.* Retrieved from ttps://vimeo.com/150308172

Chapter 9

1. WikiQuote. *Isaac Newton.* Retrieved from https://en.wiki quote.org/wiki/Isaac_Newton

2. IMDb. *Rudy: Quotes.* Retrieved from http://www.imdb.com /title/tt0108002/quotes

3. Goodreads. *Quotable Quote: Maya Angelou.* Retrieved from http://www.goodreads.com/quotes/5934-i-ve-learned-that-people-will-forget-what-you-said-people

4. Waller, Bruce. *BeALifter Interviews.* Retrieved from https:// brucewaller.wordpress.com/

5. Events for Change. *The Starfish Story: one step towards changing the world.* Retrieved from https://eventsforchange.wordpress.com/ 2011/06/05/the-starfish-story-one-step-towards-changing-the-world/

6. Goodreads. *Quotable Quote: John F. Kennedy.* Retrieved from http://www.goodreads.com/quotes/42653-we-must-find-time-to-stop-and-thank-the-people

Chapter 10

1. Successories. *Excellence Quotes.* Retrieved from http://www. successories.com/iquote/category/1133/excellence-quotes/1

2. Gleason, Steve. *Someday is Today.* Retrieved from https://twitter.com/teamgleason/status/794049222547042304

3. Maxwell, John. *Making the Tough Call.* Audio cassette. Maximum Impact Club.

4. Maxwell, John C. *The 21 Irrefutable Laws of Leadership.* Nashville: Thomas Nelson, 1998.

5. Hardy, Darren. *The Compound Effect.* New York: Vanguard Press, 2010.

, John and Jamison, Steve. *Leadership Game Plan for* :Graw-Hill, 2009.

ony. *Strategic Acceleration: Succeed at the Speed of Light.*
Brilliance o, 2009.

8. Great Inspirational Quotes. *Motivational Zig Ziglar Quotes.* Retrieved from https://www.pinterest.com/pin/189573465534957318/

9. Hardy, Darren. *The Compound Effect.* New York: Vanguard Press, 2010.

10. Gladwell, Malcolm. *Outliers.* New York: Little, Brown and Company, 2008.

11. Quotefancy. *10 Wallpapers: Jim Rohn.* Retrieved from https://quotefancy.com/quote/838207/Jim-Rohn-What-is-easy-to-do-is-also-easy-not-to-do

12. Goodreads. *Quotable Quote: Benjamin Franklin.* Retrieved from http://www.goodreads.com/quotes/24824-an-investment-in-knowledge-always-pays-the-best-interest

13. Bowman, Bob. *The Golden Rules: 10 Steps to World-Class Excellence in Your Life and Work.* New York: St. Martin's Press, 2016.

Conclusion

1. The Quotable Coach. *"A bad attitude is like a flat tire, you can't go anywhere until you change it!"* Retrieved from http://www.thequotablecoach.com/flat-tire/

2. Maxwell, John C. *The 21 Irrefutable Laws of Leadership.* Nashville: Thomas Nelson, 1998.

3. Bible Gateway. *Proverbs 27:17:* Retrieved from https://www.biblegateway.com/passage/?search=Proverbs%2027:17

4. Goodreads. *Wilferd Peterson Quotes.* Retrieved from https://www.goodreads.com/author/quotes/707594.Wilferd_Peterson